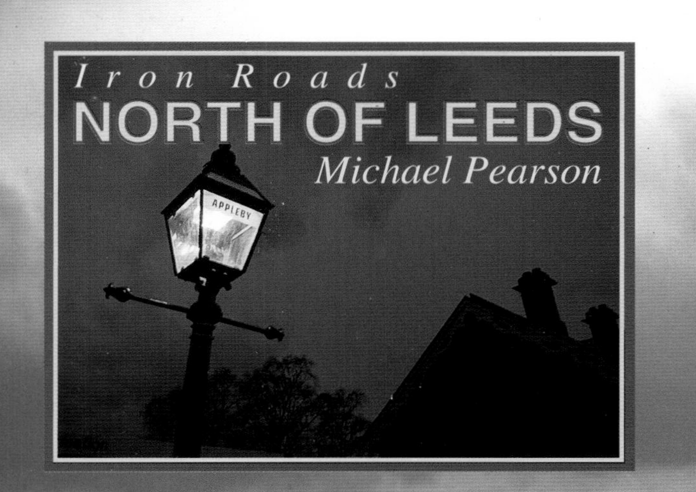

www.wayzgoose.org.uk Tel: 01283 713674 / 821472

First Edition 2004 ISBN 0 9545383 5 8
Printed in Italy by STIGE Via Pescarito 110
10099 San Mauro

KIRKBY STEPHEN

WAYZGOOSE

BETWEEN THE LINES

David Alison

HEAVEN forbid that I would ever subscribe to Lady Bracknell's view* that 'the line is immaterial'. Wildean wit is all very well, but for me - and for, I suspect, the majority of readers of this book - the line is everything: heritage, topography, engineering and architecture all rolled into one character-defining, pleasure-deriving, life-enriching permanent way.

IRON ROADS NORTH OF LEEDS features three lines which are about as far as it is possible to get from the dictionary definition of immaterial. All three are of unequivocable historic significance, and they are all so different in character from one another as to defy categorisation: though in broad terms one is now a backwater, another a revitalised trunk route, and the third a thriving commuter line. You don't have to be a card-carrying rail buff to have heard of the Settle & Carlisle - as upwards of half a million boggle-eyed tourists perennially affirm - but the routes from Leeds to Morecambe and Leeds to York via Harrogate are more esoterically enjoyed, and this book breaks new ground in holding them up to the appreciation of a wider public.

TRADITIONALLY, Yorkshire's West Riding inhabitants have enjoyed a perhaps surprising affinity with the Lancashire coast - more particularly Morecambe - where one might have expected a mill-workers holiday exodus to make a bee-line for their home county's resorts of Bridlington, Filey and Scarborough: the sometimes apparently random provision of a railway over

*The Importance Of Being Earnest

Coaling and watering a steam charter at Appleby

a century and a half ago, often remains an influence on travel patterns to this day.

In this case it was one of the north of England's lesser known railway concerns, the so-called 'Little' North Western Railway, which forged a link between Airedale and the Lancashire seaside, as part of its development of a through line north from Skipton towards Carlisle: difficulties with the development of this route eventually resulted in construction of the Settle & Carlisle.

But it wasn't only holidaymakers who found the line conducive. In its heyday a 'Residential' express ran so that the wool magnates of Bradford could commute between the coast and their palatial offices in 'Little Germany'.

Regrettably, in these utilitarian times, there are no longer any comfortable express trains to take you from Leeds to Lancaster and Morecambe. But the diesel units which provide today's services do introduce you to an enjoyable slice of the North Country; the former textile towns of the West Riding giving way to the delightful dales-like countryside of the Wenning Valley, followed by associations with Brief Encounter at Carnforth, and then the historic county town of Lancaster, before you reach the famous sunset-staging backdrop of Morecambe Bay.

Peter J. Robinson

NOT so much a railway, more a national monument, the Settle & Carlisle has survived as many assassination attempts as the leader of a Third World junta to become a nationally known visitor attraction capable of supporting its very own hinterland of a vibrant tourist-based economy.

Built, three-quarters of the way through the 19th century, across some of the bleakest landscapes in Europe, its very origins owed more to a misplaced spirit of competition than sound

The return of locomotive-hauled services to the Settle & Carlisle has been welcomed by tourists and enthusiasts alike. Here, a pair of EWS Class 37s 'top & tail' an afternoon Carlisle to Leeds train past Ais Gill under the flank of Whernside.

A Cumbria Classic Coaches 1951 Guy Arab runs past Dandry Mire Viaduct, Garsdale. Vintage buses link Kirkby Stephen with Ribblehead on Summer Tuesdays.

financial judgment. And yet, once it had been constructed - its mighty viaducts hurled across ravines, its tunnels penetrating the obstinate limestone cores of numerous fells - it enjoyed the best part of a century of strategic importance until British Rail began to bleat like moorland sheep about the haemorrhaging cost of its upkeep. Throughout the 1980s they argued for its closure, and yet the louder they thumped the tub the more passenger numbers grew, inversely attracted by the negative publicity. Public support for the line's retention - admirably channeled and focussed by the Friends of the Settle & Carlisle Line - climaxed with the Government refusing to consent to the closure proposal in 1989.

To their credit, British Rail responded not by sulking, but by promoting development of the line and modernising its passenger services. What they could not have foreseen was that, post privatisation, it should develop as a strategic route for heavy freight, notably in the carriage of coal from Scotland - much of it imported from abroad - to Yorkshire and the English midlands. With upwards of fifteen 2,000 tonne coal trains traversing the line each day - operated by EWS, Freightliner, and possibly also Jarvis in the future - track and infrastructure upgrades became a necessity. Railtrack and Network Rail have spent over £50 million towards this end, adopting 'blockade' closure techniques during the winter months to facilitate progress as rapidly and as cost-effectively as possible. Thus, having escaped from total closure by the skin of its teeth, the Settle & Carlisle is now enjoying a new lease of life, and in doing so illustrating just how wasteful other controversial post-Beeching closures, such as the Waverley, the East Lincs and the Woodhead routes have proved.

YOU shouldn't be misled by the departure board's insistence that an hourly service departs from Leeds to a place called Poppleton - or for that matter from York to Burley Park - this is just the train operator's insurance against passengers wishing to go from Leeds to York (and vice versa) via the direct 25 mile route from boarding those trains which take an Irish sense of delight in travelling the long way round, making their way via Harrogate, a little matter of 39 miles. But - as in many aspects of life - speed is not necessarily a synonym for what is good and what is best, and if only in terms of scenic interest and railway history, the Leeds-Harrogate-York route has a good deal going for it.

The apparently wayward nature of the route is explained by the fact it was the work of two separate railway companies in the mid 19th century: the Leeds & Thirsk Railway opened as a main line to the north in 1849; and the East & West Yorkshire Junction Railway, a more modest branchline designed to link York with Harrogate, which was completed two years later. Only in recent years has the route been worked as one with an intensity of service unimagined in the past. New stations have broadened the line's appeal to commuters, though the rushed closures of the Beeching era resulted in the regretted abandonment of what would have been immensely useful routes north of Harrogate to Ripon and Northallerton, and rail links with the growing dormitory towns of Wetherby and Otley.

The 'long way round' between Leeds and York has much to commend it: beyond Bramhope Tunnel the train runs through the beautiful countryside of Lower Wharfedale; at Knaresborough it soars high above the River Nidd on a classically styled viaduct; whilst eastwards across the Vale of York it becomes a delightful throwback with traditionally-gated level-crossings, timber-built signal boxes and token working. What better way of getting to the National Railway Museum? Make the most of this old fashioned railway line while it lasts.

THE importance of our railways, and the contribution they can make to transport in our grid-locked island, has never been less in doubt: their limitations are their very strengths. Unlike the car and the lorry they cannot go anywhere, a blessing too often misinterpreted as a failing. Car clubs, cycle hire and learning to walk again are literally the ways forward. In return, all we would ask is that the Train Operating Companies give us comfortable, passenger-friendly trains - not so much a lost art, as a mislaid one. Arriva Northern's introduction of a locomotive-hauled service from Knaresborough via Leeds to Carlisle in the Autumn of 2003 gave us back leg-room, window views, luggage space, and a guard's van capable of carrying bicycles. Trains, it may be necessary to remind 21st century design and procurement teams, are not aeroplanes that run on rails.

Get out there and follow in my tracks. Mine are the public transports of a private man - you will have your own incentives, make your own discoveries, cherish your own memories. The trick is not only to leave the car behind and go by train, but to get out as often as possible and explore the world beyond the far end of 'Station Road'. As the sign says ...

Michael Pearson

Penyghent looms over the foot-crossing at the southern end of Horton-in-Ribblesdale station

Leeds Carnforth Morecambe

Keighley

Leeds

Carnforth

ALMOST a quarter of a billion pounds was spent on the rebuilding of Leeds station, completed in 2002. Four years worth of work to remodel a dispiriting structure and increasingly congested layout dating from the 1960s; the former 'City' station, itself an amalgamation of the 'Wellington' and 'New' stations previously belonging to the Midland and London & North Western and North Eastern railway companies respectively.

Nowadays, upwards of sixty thousand passengers per day enjoy the benefits of extra platforms (12 to 17) and segregated running lines. Gleaming and silvered and hi-tech, the revitalised station resembles a vast retail warehouse, functional in the extreme, yet it is difficult to evade the ironic suspicion that the most aesthetically pleasing part of the station is the refurbished north concourse of 1930s Art Deco origin.

Trains for Skipton and beyond, as well as York via Harrogate, depart from platforms 1-6 and accelerate quickly over the complex pointwork of the station's western approaches, offering glimpses over the River Aire and the Leeds & Liverpool Canal, companions on the journey through Airedale to Gargrave and beyond. Then, as the train crosses the urban motorway in the vicinity of the old Holbeck station (which had lower and upper levels; the latter connecting with the Great Northern Railway's 'Central' station closed in 1967) you can look down on a former roundhouse engine shed and crescent-shaped repair shed dating from the dawn of the railway era; the roundhouse now finding use, not quite so romantically, as a depot for a van rental firm. Beyond, in amongst a constantly burgeoning number of modern multi-storey buildings, are the University's Portland stone Parkinson building, the slender, golden owl-topped spires of the Civic Hall and the tower of Cuthbert Broderick's splendid Town Hall.

Overlooked by the castellated ramparts of Armley Gaol, the line burrows through deep cuttings of stone retaining walls bearing the patina of soot left behind by generations of steam trains, past Wortley Junction and the line to Harrogate (Map 18) and past the site of Armley (Canal Road) station, closed along with other stops between Leeds and Shipley in 1965. The line between Leeds and Shipley was opened by the Leeds & Bradford Railway in 1846. The route had been surveyed by George Stephenson who favoured the easier, though longer course through the Aire Valley; 14 miles compared with 10 across the hills by way of Pudsey. The Midland Railway took over the Leeds & Bradford in 1851. During the rest of the 19th century traffic grew and steps were taken to widen

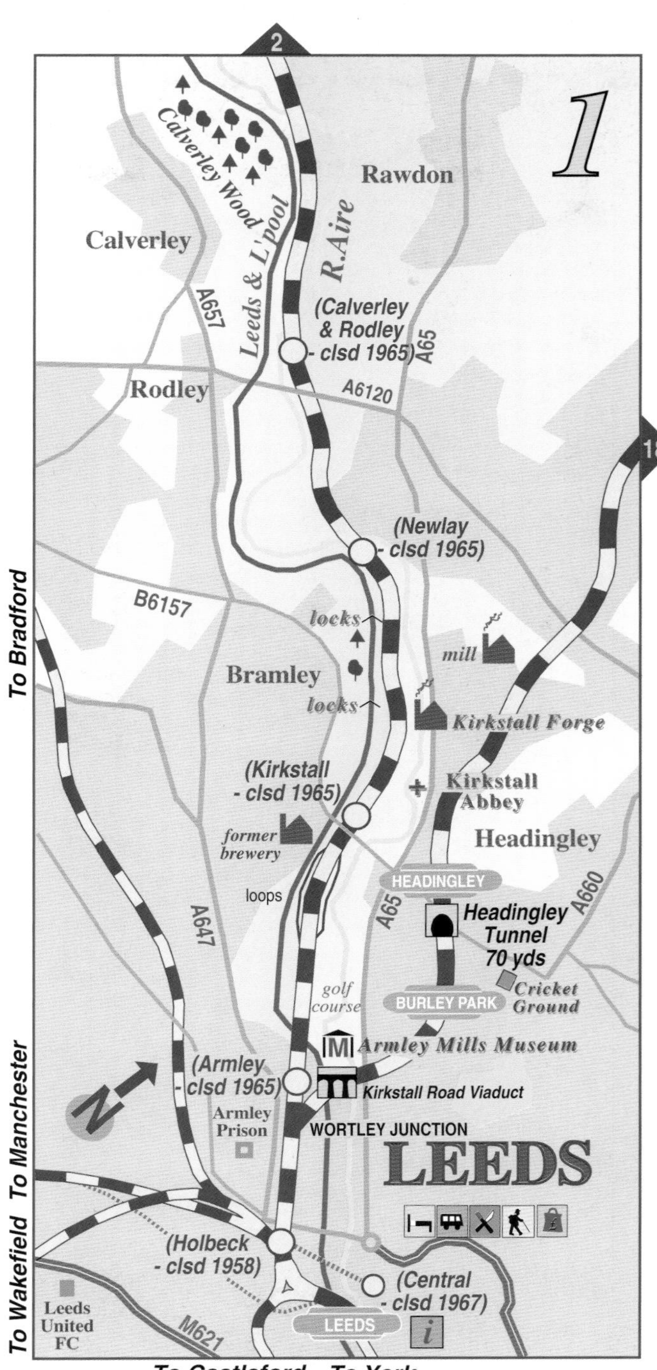

the existing two tracks into four. Most of this quadrupling has reverted to double track again, though loops remain at Kirkstall to enable a growing number of goods trains to be overtaken.

At KIRKSTALL a fly-over was built to carry the fast lines over the slow ones, but this was demolished in 1967. From the western side of the train you can catch a glimpse of a basin where canal barges (or 'keels') with electrically inspired names like *Arc* and *Relay* unloaded cargoes of coal for the power station which stood alongside the railway on the opposite side of the tracks, its site now occupied by a golf course.

The present Kirkstall Bridge dates from 1912, its ironwork cast locally at Stanningley. An earlier bridge across the Aire at this point was deliberately destroyed by a group of Royalists during the Civil War to delay the Parliamentarian march on Leeds. Up on the hillside to the west stands the old Kirkstall Brewery now converted into student accommodation. During the 1950s this was where the famous Mackeson stout was brewed. Earlier in the 20th century keels carried much of the Kirkstall Brewery's output in hogsheads along the Leeds & Liverpool Canal and Aire & Calder Navigation to Goole for export aboard its own steamships.

In lineside fields, now adapted as sports grounds, rhubarb was nurtured in large quantities. Once a nightly 'rhubarb express' left Leeds for Covent Garden, but now the focus of Yorkshire rhubarb growing has shifted towards Wakefield. The rhubarb was kept out in the fields for a couple of years before being taken into the darkened, heated 'forcing sheds'; as it ripened it was said to 'sing'.

Beyond the fields stands Kirkstall Abbey, founded by a Cistercian order of monks in 1152. For almost four centuries the order went about its austere and silent routine on the banks of the Aire until Henry VIII brought about the Dissolution. By the 18th century the abbey was no more than a romantic ruin, a source of inspiration for poets and painters alike: Turner painted the view here in 1824. In contrast to the faded pomp of the abbey, Kirkstall Forge - which dates as far back as the 17th century - continues to thrive as a centre for the manufacture of commercial vehicle axles.

After Newlay the line begins to shake free of the suburbs and move out into open countryside, passing the site of Calverley & Rodley station which if re-opened, one imagines, would make an excellent park & ride railhead, especially given its proximity to Leeds' ring-road.

APPERLEY JUNCTION lies 202 miles from the Midland Railway's London terminus, St Pancras. Here the direct line to Ilkley diverges on its way up into Wharfedale. Apperley Viaduct was swept away by the swollen waters of the Aire in 1866. Nearby a line once led into Esholt's huge sewage works which had its own internal railway system, its locomotives making environmentally sound use of waste oils from wool products as a fuel. Esholt is perhaps better known these days as the filming location for the television soap *Emmerdale*.

Between Apperley and Shipley the River Aire curves northwards in a wide arc around a bluff of high ground. The canal builders followed suit, but the more confident and technically accomplished railway engineers were not going to be deflected so easily. The resulting THACKLEY TUNNEL is almost a mile long. A second bore was built when the line was quadrupled and this is the one in use today.

Cheek by jowl stand the old textile towns of Shipley, Saltaire and Bingley, their factory chimneys perforating the Pennine sky in a salute to Victorian energy and arrogance. But these often flamboyantly ornate perpendicular monuments to trade form a petrified forest now, and smoke no longer billows into the West Riding sky in a visual affirmation of a prosperity that has vanished, to be replaced by the high-tech industries of the 21st century. Once the line has emerged from the gloom of Thackley Tunnel it is rejoined by the river and the canal. Slipping down the hillside comes the trackbed of the Great Northern Railway's positively Alpine branch line from Bradford - closed to passenger trains as early as 1931 - to terminate in a not unhandsome stone station building now in light industrial use.

SHIPLEY is a rare triangular station. Electrification and resignalling of the local network has rid it of its extensive cast-iron canopies and timber signal boxes, but it was refurbished by Railtrack in 1998 and the booking hall, particularly, remains of interest. The triangular arrangement of the platforms permits trains to run through to Bradford from Ilkley, Leeds and Skipton in addition to services on the main line; though provision of platforms on the direct Leeds-Skipton route did not occur until 1979 on the ‘down’ line and 1992 on the ‘up’.

Barely gathering any semblance of speed from their stop at Shipley, northbound stopping trains brake for SALTAIRE, a former model village created by Sir Titus Salt to house his workers in the massive mill adjacent to the line. Look out on

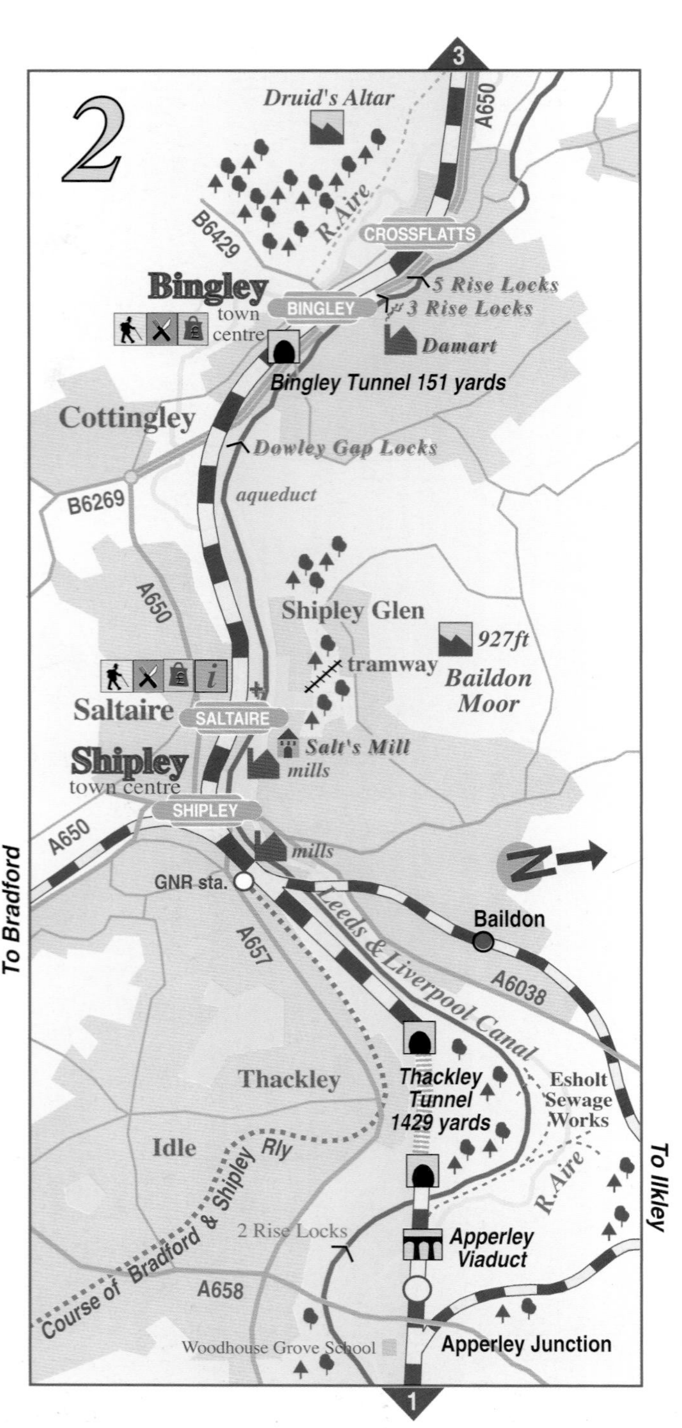

the corner of the old engine house for the engraved alpaca, a sort of llama whose wool was much used in the mill.

Saltaire station was re-opened under the auspices of Metro in 1984, and when you alight you step not just on to the platform, but back in time as well, for the whole of Saltaire seems caught in a time warp, as though the present century is just a bad dream from which you had awoken back into the more measured pace of the 1880s. Every attempt was made with the new station to perpetuate this illusion. There are imitation gas lamps, Midland look-alike diagonal fencing, flower baskets and trim stone waiting shelters.

Saltaire has another railway which you should take the time to go and ride on. The Shipley Glen Tramway dates from 1895, which makes it the oldest cable operated tramway in the British Isles. It climbs for about a quarter of a mile through delightful woodland, carpeted with wood anemones and bluebells in Spring. Each 'train' is made up of two carriages - one open and one covered. The journey takes little more than two or three minutes, but the experience has a magical quality about it which has endeared itself to generations of West Riding folk. At the top you can visit a splendidly old-fashioned fun fair - which still has 'tuppenny' slot machines, visit the Bracken Hall Countryside Centre or wander further up on to the edge of the moors.

Reminders of Sir Titus Salt's altruism are evident as the train passes sports grounds still bearing his name. Canal and railway cross the Aire at Dowley Gap and, in turn, the railway crosses a new dual-carriageway which has gone some way to relieving the chronic traffic problems of the Aire Valley.

Blocks of high rise flats herald the approach to BINGLEY. Stone built and substantial, the Midland obviously regarded this as a stop of some importance, though nowadays there is a slightly forlorn feel to the station, part of which is used by a dancing school: rumbas and tangos where they once pasted labels on the left luggage. Long years after work first commenced, a new dual-carriageway now squeezes its way between the railway and the canal. Damart's famous thermal underwear works occupies a huge mill overlooking a substantial 3-Rise lock on the canal. A little further on, stands the 5-Rise - one of the 'Seven Wonders of the Waterways' - a stunning feat of 19th century engineering more easily appreciated from the train in winter when the surrounding foliage is at its least dense. Better still, alight at either Bingley or Crossflatts and take an enjoyable walk along the towpath to see the canal at closer hand.

Titus Salt's gargantuan Italianate alpaca mill at Saltaire, now filled with classy shops, galleries and restaurants

Steaming up into the Worth Valley - an Ivatt
2-6-2 tank leaves Keighley for Oxenhope

EITHER side of the line ridges etched by stone walling rise to meet moorlands which, for the northbound traveller, anticipate the scenic splendours to come. The dual-carriageway and a sewage works do what they can to poop the party, whilst a pair of gasholders prevent all but a distant glimpse of the 17th century National Trust property, East Riddlesden Hall. In a moment or two Keighley's industry will impinge, but there is every indication that the railway is beginning to escape from the conventional image of the West Riding and find its way out into the Broad Acres of another kind of Yorkshire altogether.

Like the old football cliche, KEIGHLEY is a station of 'two halves'. The configuration is unusual - two separate pairs of platforms laid out in a shallow V shape. Metro's side of the station has been refurbished, the roomy booking hall with its Midland seating and airy skylight taking pride of place. The other half of the station belongs to the Keighley & Worth Valley Railway whose five mile branch line climbs assiduously out of this landscape of mills and foundries up into the resonant textures of Bronteland. Thus, at Keighley, the diesel and electric trains of the present day come face to face with their forbears; vintage steam locomotives and carriages which are the images of childhood. Somewhere up in the Worth Valley the Railway Children are eternally at play in the imagination of us all. And even if the Worth Valley local isn't waiting lazily at its platform, steam licking round its coupling rods, the lovingly kept station, with its posters vouchsafing the charms of long forgotten holiday resorts, hints at glories up the single line to Haworth and Oxenhope that are difficult to resist.

The Aire Valley trains, however, make a quick getaway from Keighley, treating you to fleeting glimpses, barely retained, of textile works, dye factories, engineering plants and foundries; the lifeblood of the town, tens of thousands of livelihoods; all those people trying to keep the balls of their juggling act in the air while you swan superciliously past on the train.

The line you are travelling on was promoted by the Leeds & Bradford Railway as an extension from Shipley to Colne. Skipton was reached in 1847, Colne the following year. This part of the Aire Valley offered fairly easy running - the line falls towards STEETON & SILSDEN at 1 in 247 then climbs to the site of Kildwick & Crosshills station (closed in 1965) at 1 in 338. Flicking through the pages of old railway journals, the timing logs presented by the likes of Cecil J. Allen and O.S.

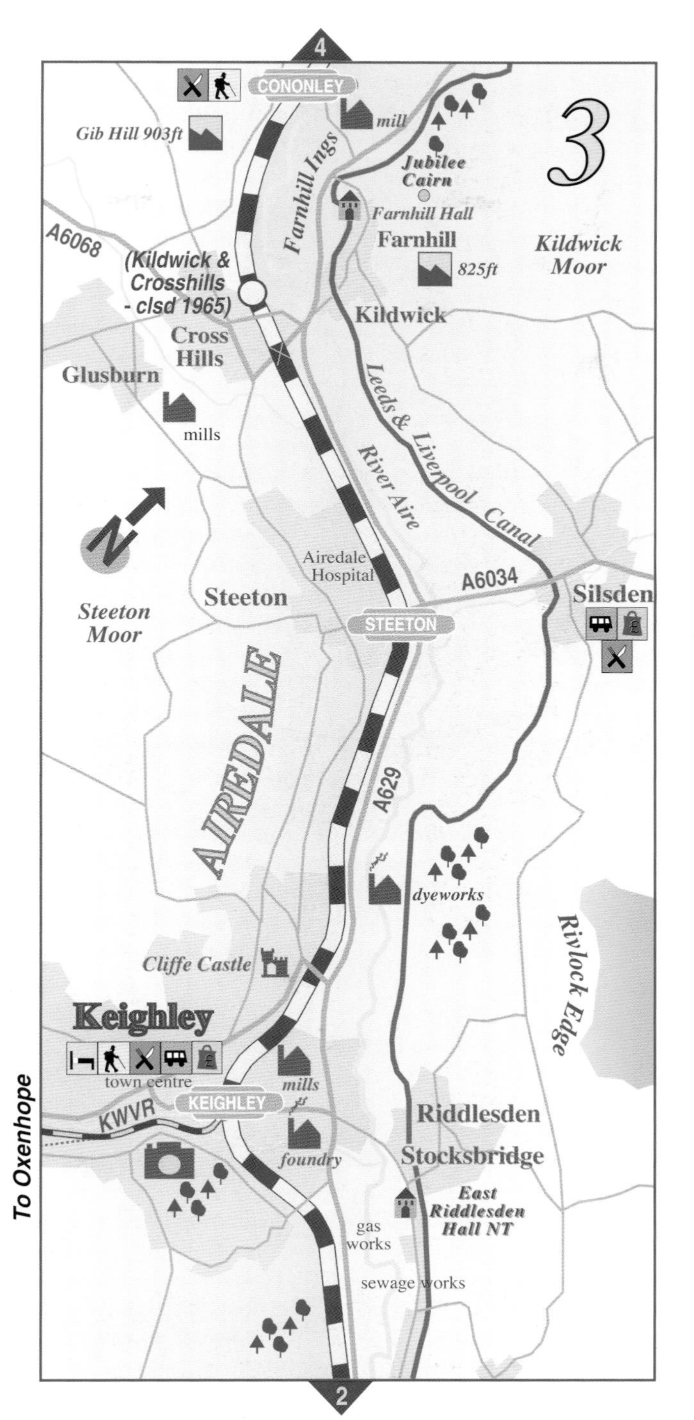

Nock reveal that steaming was easy on this stretch, and that the "Thames-Clyde Express" and "The Waverley" (St Pancras to Glasgow and Edinburgh respectively) were easily capable of 'a mile a minute' along here.

Like a wing three-quarter who's spotted a likely opening, the railway executes a neat shimmy and heads for the Aire Gap. A sense of impetus multiplies, but there are still Metro halts to impede the progress of most trains. STEETON & SILSDEN was re-opened in 1988. Just past the station Damart have another factory, and then you can see the vast Airedale Hospital on the same side. A mile further on the line crosses the boundary between West and North Yorkshire. To the west you can see the chimney of an old lead mine on Gib Hill. To the east, sheltered by a mask of trees, stands Farnhill Hall. It dates from the 12th century and has four battlemented towers: defence against deep incursions by the border 'reivers'.

Just next to Farnhill Hall, a typical hump-backed bridge marks the presence of the Leeds & Liverpool Canal. One of three Trans-Pennine canals dating from the 18th century, the Leeds & Liverpool is 127 miles long with 91 locks. It was built to wide-beam dimensions and the barges, or 'short-boats' which plied its waters measured 14ft wide by 62ft in length. The record time for a horse-drawn passage over the entire length of the canal dates from 1944, when a cargo of sugar was carried from Tate & Lyle in Liverpool to Leeds Basin in 52 hours. These days the canal is given over entirely to pleasure traffic and, by sheer coincidence, the publishers of this guide also produce one to the canal: *Pearson's Canal Companion - Pennine Waters*; £7.95 (Tel: 01788 546692).

Strangely, when one considers its rural setting, CONONLEY retains its railway station. Not that we should be anything but grateful, for this is one of those bewitching wayside platforms which seem to almost compel one to leave the train and melt into the landscape. Such qualities are difficult to define, but you know them when you feel them. Here, perhaps, it's the simplicity which beguiles. Past a dignified mill a by-road crosses the Aire leading to the escarpment of Bradley Moor, topped by a whitewashed cairn commemorating Queen Victoria's Jubilee in 1887. In the opposite direction the road winds through the village, ascends on to Cononley Moor, then swoops down into the loneliness of Lothersdale, a remote valley threaded by the Pennine Way. It is difficult to accept that Lancashire lies only five miles to the west.

ON either side of the valley floor, hills begin to ride in waves on the horizon. The Aire, with built up banks, meanders through the marshy terrain of Bradley Ings; 'ings' being Yorkshire-speak for ground susceptible to flooding. Hereabouts the river has journeyed about a dozen miles from its source at Malham and has another seventy or so to go to its confluence with the Ouse upstream of Goole. The adjoining hillsides, sprinkled with sturdy farms and patterned by drystone walls begin to have the look of The Dales about them. Not the concerto let alone the symphony yet, perhaps, but the overture at least!

SKIPTON station has enjoyed a new lease of life with electrification of the Airedale line. Set on a graceful curve, its handsome canopies are decked out in green and blue and gold colours; the decorative ironwork as delicate as lace. Spruced up, its creamy stone buildings have regained much of their original Midland Railway dignity. Above the entrance to the booking hall the Midland's hallmark of a 'wyvern' still grimaces down on prospective passengers. Frequent electric trains begin and end their journeys here, whilst interludes of silence are broken by the hubbub of Craven-accented conversations.

There used to be two more platforms catering for trains to Ilkley via Addingham, a route closed back in 1965. But if commuters can no longer travel directly to Ilkley, at least part of that lovely line has been restored and reopened by the Embsay & Bolton Abbey Railway. A branch of that branch led to Grassington and is still used, as far as Rylstone for the extraction of locally quarried limestone by rail, though there are suggestions that a passenger service might be reinstated at some point in the future.

The line northwards from Skipton was promoted by a company called the North Western and work began on the route in 1846. Railway mania was at its height and this modest outfit - who had no connection with the then recently formed giant, the London & North Western - had an eye on developing traffic between the West Riding and Scotland by linking Skipton with the Lancaster to Carlisle line. With hindsight the 'Little North Western' (as it became known in deference to the LNWR) was like a difficult piece in a jigsaw, a cause and effect with ramifications scarcely guessed at when the route was planned. Over the next twenty years the line became a battleground between the powerful Midland and London & North Western railways, and a root cause in the Midland's eventual decision to build its own direct line to Scotland; the Settle & Carlisle. Pulling away from Skipton you pass the former engine shed now used as an industrial unit - and, going under the by-pass, you see the trackbed of the line to Colne threading its way disconsolately across the valley floor at the foot of Elsack Moor. Dismantled railways exude their own particular brand of melancholy and more often than not their loss seems such a waste. The line from Skipton to Colne was closed in 1970, severing a through route between West Yorks and East Lancs which had played a useful role in local communications for 120 years. What blinkered act of post-Beeching book-keeping justified such a closure? The stations at Skipton and Colne remain open, but the track between, just eleven miles of railway, has vanished. Still, despite the interruption and confusion of privatisation, there is no such thing as a lost cause in railway terms and re-opening of the route is being actively campaigned for.

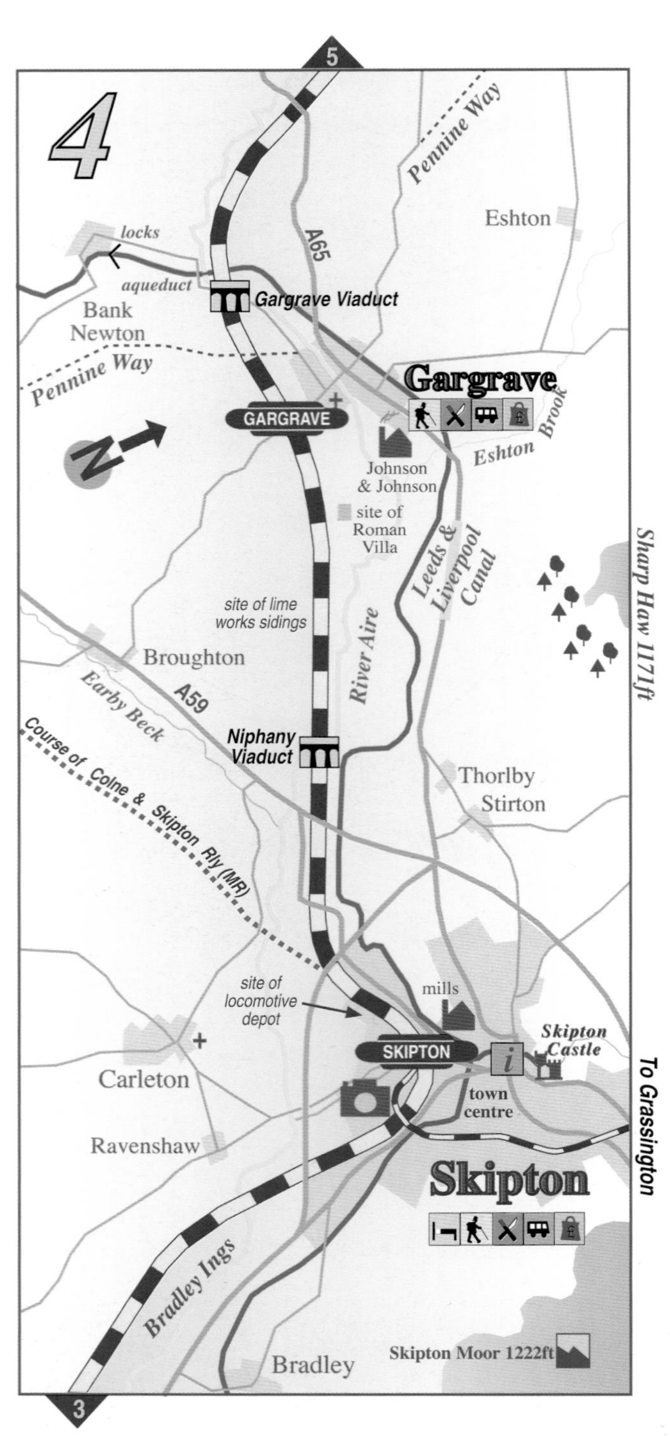

Out from Skipton you soon emerge into a fresh landscape where mills are finally absent. With the Aire, and Leeds & Liverpool Canal keeping company with the railway, there are views north-eastwards to the forested flank of Sharp Haw and a hint of higher fells beyond. You are now in the Craven District of North Yorkshire, an ancient name derived from the Celtic for 'land of crags'. Gritstone has given way to limestone.

Crossing the Aire by way of the sweetly-named Niphany Viaduct, where if you're going slowly enough you might just glimpse a trout or two swimming, the train passes rough ground once laid out with sidings serving a lime works. Johnson & Johnson's 'wound management' works dominates the middle ground to the east. Under the lawn in the garden of a house beside the line there's a Roman mosaic floor.

GARGRAVE station emphasises the change in origin of the railway which occurred back at Skipton. The old booking hall, converted into a private residence, is in a half-timbered style typical of the Little North Western. Look out for the milepost on the up platform - 225 miles from London St Pancras!

Look out in the adjacent fields for back-packers trudging along the Pennine Way, then keep your eyes peeled for a glimpse of canal boats as the railway says a fond hail or farewell to the Leeds & Liverpool Canal. It's probably taken you three-quarters of an hour to get this far by train from Leeds. By boat Leeds is twenty-four hours steady cruising and locking from Gargrave. You almost envy the boaters and walkers their snail-like progress, for the train passes too rapidly through this lovely countryside. For a mile or two the river lies on the western side of the line, indulging itself in an amazing sequence of corkscrews.

Electrification has enhanced Skipton's status as a busy commuter railhead - here a Class 333 electric unit waits to leave for Leeds

A Kirkby Thore bound gypsum train prepares to shatter Hellifield's cloistered calm

THE railway leaves the Aire behind at BELL BUSK. From here a horse omnibus carried Victorian and Edwardian ramblers to the awe-inspiring scenes of Malham Cove and Gordale Scar which Turner, the landscape artist, had been inspired to paint before the railway gave tourists more easy access to the area. In 1951 Bell Busk station was used for scenes in a long-forgotten film *Another Man's Poison* starring Bette Davis. The half-timbered, North Western style station closed in 1958 and is now a private hotel (Tel: 01729 830301), the old booking hall being used as a dining room and the bar occupying part of the former platform. Railway enthusiasts from all over the world come here to stay and watch the trains go by.

Between Bell Busk and Hellifield the railway crosses a low watershed separating the Aire and Ribble valleys. Becks which spring from neighbouring moors thus find their way haphazardly and at length into the North or Irish seas. The landscape is now of bare, sensuously rounded hills, boulder clay on limestone, known as 'The Sweetlands' because of the quality of the grazing. Irish cattle were docked at Heysham and brought by the Midland Railway to Bell Busk for fattening on these rich pastures. So too were Eden Valley lambs, apparently riding in open wagons and wrapped in hessian.

With Pendle Hill, legendary home of the Lancashire Witches, prominent to the south-west, the train arrives at HELLIFIELD. 231 miles from St Pancras, this was once a junction of some stature. Its long canopies, which have been likened to cathedral cloisters, reflect a lost significance emphasised by the abandoned bay platforms where demure branch line trains once kept timetabled assignations with the haughty Leeds-Carlisle expresses. The Lancashire & Yorkshire sent its caramel shortbread coloured carriages up the Ribble Valley from Blackburn to fraternise with the florid crimson red trains of the Midland and both companies had their own sidings, engine sheds and streets of employees housing.

In its heyday almost 70% of Hellifield's male population worked on the railway. Provision of housing by the 'Lanky' and the Midland was not so much a case of altruism as an economic necessity. Had accommodation not been forthcoming, insufficient men would have been attracted to the neighbourhood to provide a workforce for a railway centre which never went to sleep. Knocker-ups had a vital role to play in ensuring that men turned up for their shifts on time, though how they slept at all through the interminable noise of passing trains and shunting sessions

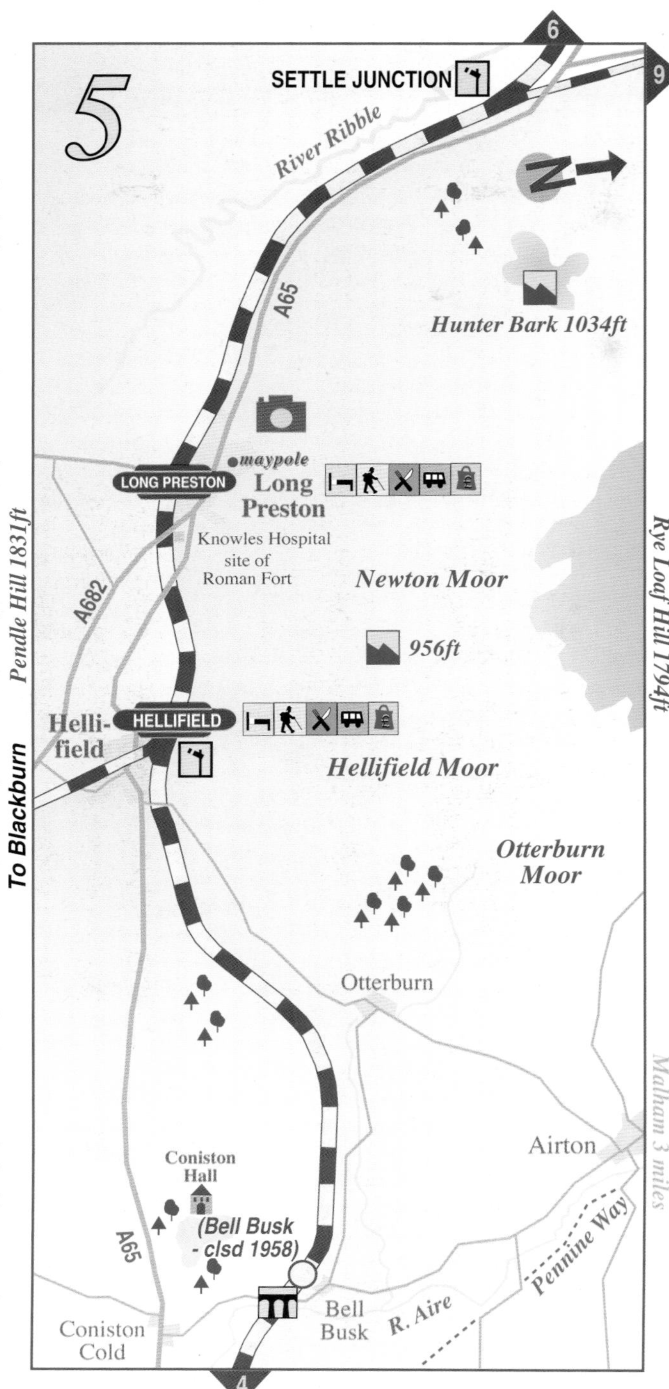

is open to conjecture.

Most of the shunting was concerned with exchange traffic between the two railways and high and low level yards lay either side of the Blackburn route adjacent to its confluence with the main line. Traffic of local origin was mostly in the shape of minerals from neighbouring quarries and livestock from Hellifield's flourishing auction mart. But it was perhaps with passengers that Hellifield was most significantly concerned. Cassells *Official Guide to the Midland Railway* of 1912 informs us that the station 'is supplied with a letter-box, a telegraph office, a bookstall, and refreshment rooms,' going on to list copiously the connections to be made with stations as disparate as Moses Gate, Turton & Edgworth, Burscough Junction, Midge Hall and Cherry Tree.

In those days almost a hundred passenger trains passed through Hellifield each day, but come the last quarter of the 20th century the station was down on its knees, its buildings in decay and serving only a handful of trains per day. Happily, its status was recognised in time and a formidable programme of regeneration returned at least the fabric of the station to good repair. Unfortunately Hellifield's projected development as a visitor centre and operating base for steam charters has so far not come to fruition. A new building to house steam locomotives remains unfinished and the cafe and shop which opened following refurbishment has shut down. There is a ghostly feel about Hellifield once again, and it would be sad if all the restoration work, so painstakingly done, turned out to be a false dawn.

Barely a mile from Hellifield lies LONG PRESTON station. Before reaching it keep an eye out for an attractive row of almshouses known as Knowles Hospital on the eastern side of the line. The Ribble's broad valley is prone to flooding hereabouts and drystone walls look strangely out of place in so level a landscape. To the north and east the limestone fells surrounding Malham come into view.

With the busy A65 in close attendance, the railway reaches SETTLE JUNCTION. Forty miles out from Leeds, everything up to now has been no more than an hors-d'oeuvre. Airedale was tasty, but no more than an appetiser for the main course, now being brought to you by the landscape's attentive waiters. Initially the Little North Western keeps to the valley floor. In contrast the Settle & Carlisle (Map 9) commences climbing at its ruling gradient of 1 in 100.

THE senior railway at SETTLE JUNCTION veers westwards, crosses the Ribble, and enters GIGGLESWICK; bare-platformed now but formerly featuring a typical Little North Western half-timbered station building. Little by name and little by nature. For in a sense the Lancaster line is a modest, small scale version of the Settle & Carlisle; gentler in its landscapes, gradients, engineering and architecture. Surprisingly, given the present paucity of traffic - no freight at all and only five return passenger trips - the route remains double-tracked when one, with passing loops, would patently suffice, though there are signalling constraints, for the route is worked as one block section all the way from Settle Junction to Carnforth!

Such cogitations may afflict the railway-minded traveller, but other passengers are more likely to be preoccupied with the passing scenery which is charmingly and characteristically Dales-like. The line climbs to its summit at milepost two hundred and thirty-seven and three-quarters from St Pancras. The underfloor diesels heave a sigh of relief! Briefly there is a glimpse to the north-east of Penyghent, before that particular horizon becomes blocked by Giggleswick Scar, then cuttings swallow up the railway and one's views are foreshortened. Some of the cuttings are grassy slopes, others more precipitous with rocks and moss. Signs of life are restricted to scattered farms and the occasional atypically gregarious grouping of a hamlet, such as ELDROTH, whose little church dates from 1627.

Ingleborough becomes visible - when not cloud covered - to the north; it's a fairly taxing but invigoratingly worthwhile six mile walk from the remote station of Clapham to the top. A flat-arched viaduct of iron and stone construction spans the River Wenning on the approach to CLAPHAM. Once this was the *other* Clapham Junction, a world away in size, significance and setting from its more famous South London namesake, but the line through Ingleton to Tebay was closed to passenger trains in 1954 and goods a dozen years later. This was the route which had been the scene of contentious connections between the Midland and London & North Western railways in the years prior to construction of the Settle & Carlisle. A viaduct, which passengers were reputedly sometimes made to walk across when changing trains, still spans the gorge-like valley of the Greta at Ingleton, whilst at Clapham the cindery trackbed, colonised by silver birch now, has been annexed agriculturally. Enjoying an elevated position, retaining its half-timbered station house and attractively windowed stone shelter, Clapham's staggered platforms are linked by a metal footbridge. On a good day weatherwise, nobody could object to a long wait on Clapham's platform for the next train, given the moorland setting.

Between Clapham and Bentham a certain wildness vitalizes the landscape as the railway and the river thread their way between Newby Moor to the north and Burn Moor to the south. Up on the flank of Burn Moor, a couple of miles from Bentham station, and straddling the Yorkshire/Lancashire border, stands the Great Stone of Fourstones, an enigmatic survivor from the Ice Age.

BENTHAM station is unexpectedly modern in appearance, its main building looking as though it was designed for Potter's Bar and consigned here by clerical error. Not that this has stopped the local community from lavishing it with care and attention. Some particularly fine murals of local scenes enliven its walls. On the south side of the line, curiously aloof from the centre of Bentham, stands St Margaret's Church whilst, across the tracks, literally and metaphorically, lies a sizeable factory bearing, in faded paintwork, the title: "Geo Angus & Co Ltd - Canvas, Hose & Belting Works." Originally one of several textile mills in the Bentham area, Angus's had come down from Newcastle-on-Tyne to occupy this site and flourished for many years before being taken over by Dunlop. Nowadays the factory has evolved into the production of fire-fighting equipment.

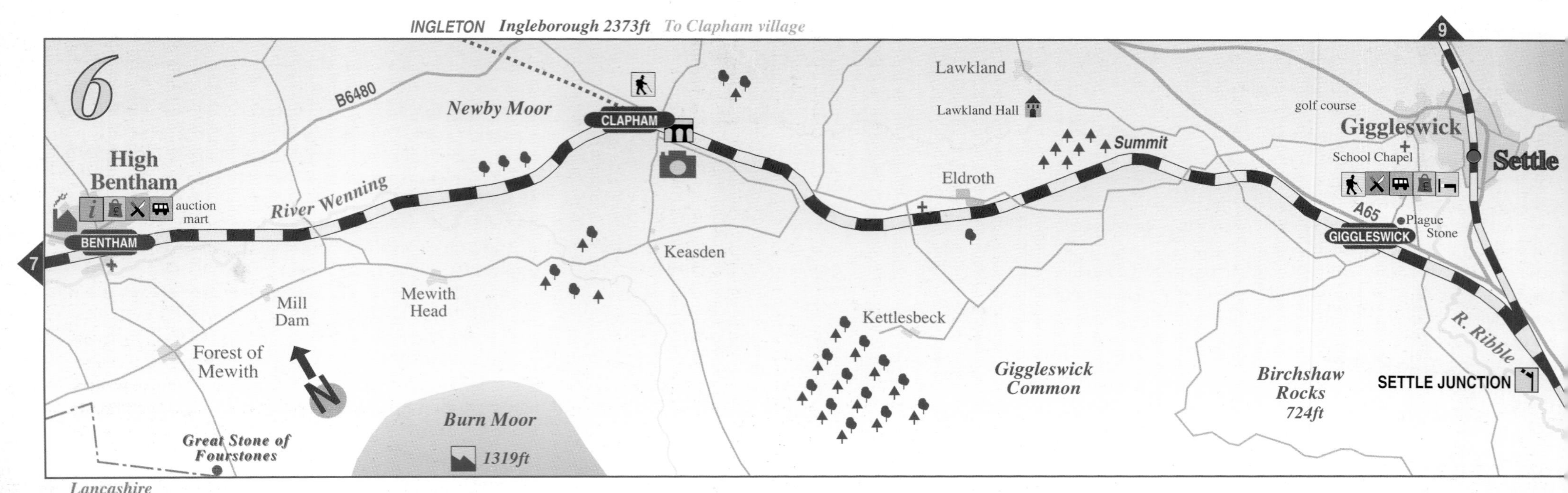

A Morecambe-bound train approaches Clapham from the east prior to crossing the River Wenning

GENERATIONS of West Riding folk rode this railway to reach 'Bradford-on-Sea', alias Morecambe. The Midland, and LMS after the grouping, ran a "Leeds, Bradford & Morecambe Residential Express" which had something of the atmosphere of a gentlemen's club about it. The 'Residential' used to leave Morecambe around half past seven in the morning and drop the wool magnates off at Bradford or Leeds just after nine. One would have relished being a fly on the empire wood of the compartment wall: who'd lowered his handicap, who'd got a new Bentley, who was raking it in, who'd been fiddling the books, who was fooling about with the svelte new parlour maid.

Passing LOW BENTHAM, which had its own passenger station in the early years of the line, and crossing the Wenning twice again, the train reaches WENNINGTON where the direct line to Lancaster and Morecambe bore south. This was the route that the holidaymakers and businessmen would have been familiar with, but it was rationalised out of existence in 1967, after which trains were diverted over the old Furness & Midland Joint line via Carnforth, adding an extra six or seven miles, and a reversal at Lancaster Castle, to the journey. The old Lune Valley route's cutting curves sadly away opposite Wennington's intact, but 'locked-out' signal cabin, a *Marie Celeste* of a Midland design which would look better for a lick of paint. This would have been a busy box in the past overseeing the splitting and joining of Carnforth and Morecambe portions which took place at Wennington.

And so the character of the railway changes yet again as the Leeds to Lancaster train moves on to metals laid to expedite the carriage of passengers and goods between industrial Yorkshire and Ireland via the ferry from Barrow to Belfast. By the beginning of the First World War, Heysham had stolen Barrow's status as the port for Belfast, but the Midland continued to run through carriages between Leeds and Bradford and Whitehaven and Windermere.

MELLING TUNNEL swallows up such thoughts before spewing the railway out into the Lune Valley which is spanned by two low-slung viaducts. The long closed wayside stations at Melling, Arkholme and Borwick display a strong family resemblance, being built of local stone. All three retain their goods sheds and all three are now in residential use.

Once across the Lune, the landscape is typified by undulating pastures sprinkled with stone built farms. The line climbs across a watershed then descends into the valley of the River Keer. Beyond Borwick the line crosses, then accompanies, the Lancaster Canal which once linked Preston with Kendal but which is no longer navigable beyond Tewitfield, the M6 having been built across its bed, though there is a strident campaign to have this crass act rectified. On the outskirts of CARNFORTH the line passes a surprisingly well preserved Midland Railway locomotive depot before rounding a tight curve towards the station. Rather surprisingly, the former Furness & Midland loop, which facilitated direct running to and from Barrow, has been lifted.

On 24th January, 1945 an advertisement in the *Morecambe Visitor* sought applications for extras in a film to be called *Brief Encounter*. It was to be night work and successful applicants were offered the lure of meals and a good remuneration. Within two weeks filming was in progress on Carnforth station, alias 'Milford Junction' in the story. Earlier in the war Carnforth had been bombed by the Germans, who recognised its strategic importance as a railway centre, but by the time the war was being won, and Carnforth no longer under threat of enemy action, it was considered an appropriate location for filming some of the scenes of *Brief Encounter*, David Lean's classic 1945 adaption of a Noel Coward story featuring Trevor Howard

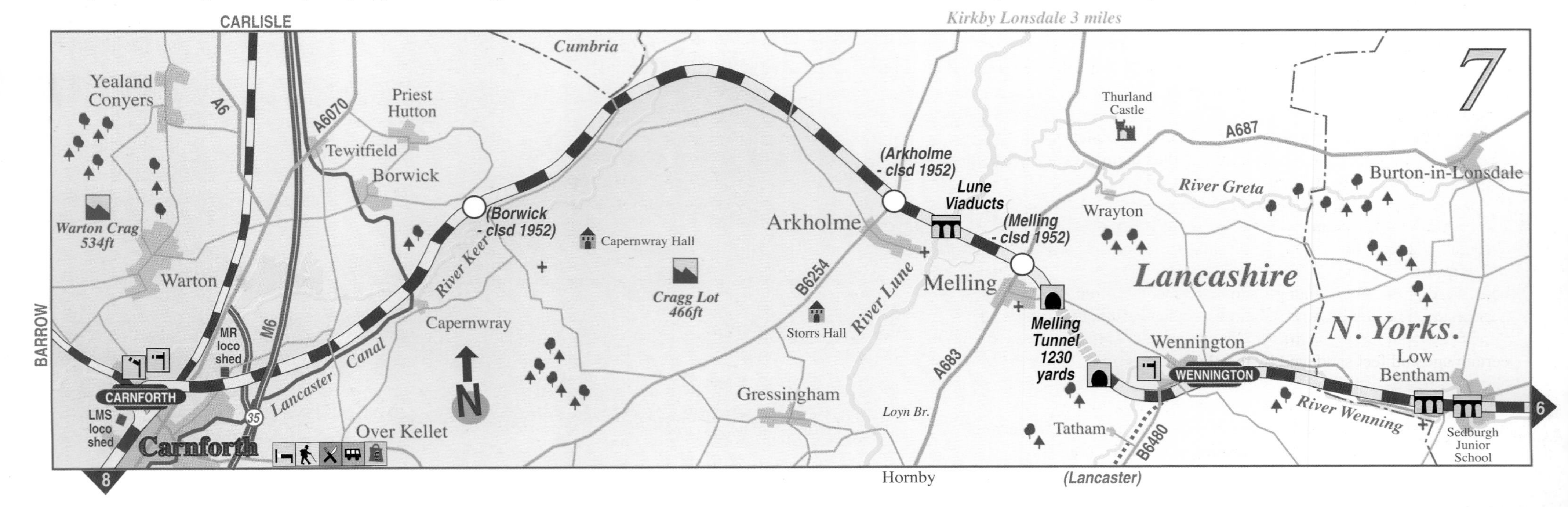

and Celia Johnson making stiff-upper-lipped love over Bath Buns to the strains of Rachmaninov's *Second Piano Concerto*. In truth Carnforth, on the fringes of the Lake District, is slightly at odds with the film's quintessentially Home Counties atmosphere. But at least it's a real England that we see on the screen and not an implausible Hollywood film set. Many of the non-railway scenes were filmed at Beaconsfield in Buckinghamshire.

It is not without irony, then, that over half a century later the film-maker's artistic licence proved the salvation of what had become, following the closure of Carnforth's important motive power depot in 1968, and the abandonment of its West Coast Main Line platforms two years later, an almost derelict and unmanned station. Yet one senses that without the fame of *Brief Encounter*, Carnforth station's admirable regeneration may never have taken place, particularly when one considers that the rebirth of the motive power depot as a visitor centre called Steamtown proved relatively shortlived.

Carnforth Station Visitor Centre & Brief Encounter Buffet Room were officially re-opened to the public in October 2003 by the only surviving member of the 1945 cast, Margaret Barton, who'd played the tea girl 'Beryl' in *Brief Encounter*. Such is the continued potency of the film that the national media descended on Carnforth for the occasion, and so effective is the recreation that you are shocked not to find Stanley Holloway leaning impudently over the counter much to the chagrin of the strait-laced manageress. Adjoining rooms have been refurbished to exhibit mementoes of Carnforth's busy railway past, and here also, history seems so tangible that you half expect the down Barrow to have transmuted itself from a Sprinter unit into a Rutherford Baltic.

By the summer of 1968, Carnforth was one of the last remaining steam motive power depots in Britain and thus the mecca of many a sad pilgrimage by railway enthusiasts from all over the world. Nowadays its premises belong to the West Coast Railway Company, and are used for the maintenance of locomotives and rolling stock engaged in charter work. Perhaps most famously now, this is the home of "Hogwart's Express", but other well known trains are also maintained here, notably the stock belonging to "The Jacobite" and the "Royal Scotsman". The coaling tower, built by Italian prisoners of war, and the smaller sanding plant, are local landmarks. And if you are of a certain age and feel saddened by the absence of grimy 'Black Fives', 'Eight Freights' and 'Standard Fours', at least draw consolation from the fact the infrastructure survives, and that from time to time the sounds of steam are still to be heard resounding off the long curving, concrete wall of Carnforth station, before heading off into the hills.

Perhaps not such a brief encounter under the clock at Carnforth

HEST BANK is the only place where the so-called West Coast Main Line actually encounters the sea, and even this can seem a slightly tenuous claim to fame when the tide is out and the waves are lapping the far side of Morecambe Bay. Hest Bank was known to holidaymakers in the Sixties for its Camping Coaches, up to five of them being berthed in a siding between the main line and the sea for hire as holiday homes. More tragically, Hest Bank recently hit the headlines as the location of the drowning of nineteen Chinese cocklers, stranded by the fast incoming rip tides of the Kent and Keer channels.

A signal box oversees use of a level crossing and the junction of the northern loop into Morecambe, used sporadically by trains carrying nuclear waste from Heysham to Sellafield, then the WCML veers inland, running parallel to the canal briefly, before becoming engulfed in the suburban outskirts of Lancaster.

A high viaduct spanning the River Lune provides rail travellers with a dramatic entry into LANCASTER. Far below, old stone-built warehouses line the tidal river reflecting a maritime prosperity long gone. Upstream you can see the Ashton Memorial nestling like a miniature St Pauls above the treetops: downstream Heysham's nuclear power station stands like a shoebox at the edge of the sea. The old Midland Railway route from Wennington through Lancaster Green Ayre to Morecambe crossed the river at a lower level and hugged the north bank as it passed beneath the West Coast Main Line. Interestingly, this line, together with the extension to Heysham, was electrified by the Midland as early as 1908.

Nowadays services between Leeds and Morecambe have to reverse out of Lancaster and retrace their inward route for a couple of miles back to Hest Bank South Junction. But with luck the timetable may spare you a few minutes to look round Lancaster's handsome station, designed by Sir William Tite in 1846, and you will see that he appeared to take his cue from the adjacent medieval castle, creating a sympathetic pastiche of its towers and battlements.

Back at Hest Bank South Junction the Morecambe line bears west and you are soon trundling into BARE LANE, a suburban station with two platforms, and a working signal box, together with a small stone station building, despondently boarded up. This route into Morecambe was built by the London & North Western Railway and originally terminated in their own station called Euston Road. Bungalows and semi-detached villas offering bed & breakfast create an impending sense of the seaside.

Abruptly, you reach the end of the line at a truncated terminus opened as recently as 1995. The gloomy gable end of a nearby building advertises 'Modern Dancing' in faded lettering, and the heart sinks. Architecturally, the new MORECAMBE station has more in keeping with the adjoining Burger King than the handsome terminus provided by the Midland a few hundred yards further on. But at least there is a booking hall and, on alighting, one is still assailed by the same quickening of pulse as generations of day-trippers and holidaymakers before us. It must be the ozone, it certainly isn't, as far as railway enthusiasts are concerned, the now stranded 'Promenade' station left behind by the rationalisations of 1995. Perhaps we should be grateful that it has been 'saved'. But a pub, an arts centre and a tourist information desk lack the dignity of the old days. Another of the walking wounded stands just across the road, facing the sea. This is the "Midland Hotel" opened by the LMS in stunning 'Art Deco' style in the Thirties. Happily, following a period of uncertainty as to its future - during which some Philistines on the local council even called for its demolition - Urban Splash - the team who did so much to regenerate run down parts of inner Manchester - have submitted plans to refurbish the Midland to its former glory with speciality retail outlets and even an open-air heated bathing pool on the roof.

Our survey of the line from Leeds ends here, but it's worth mentioning that, twice a day, trains still trundle round the loop to HEYSHAM to connect with the Isle of Man ferry. Heysham was developed as a port by the Midland Railway, primarily as a link with Belfast to which sailings began in 1904. In Midland days the "Belfast Boat Express" would leave St Pancras at teatime and run via Sheffield and Leeds to catch the midnight sailing from Heysham which docked at Belfast's Donegall Quay around six the following morning.

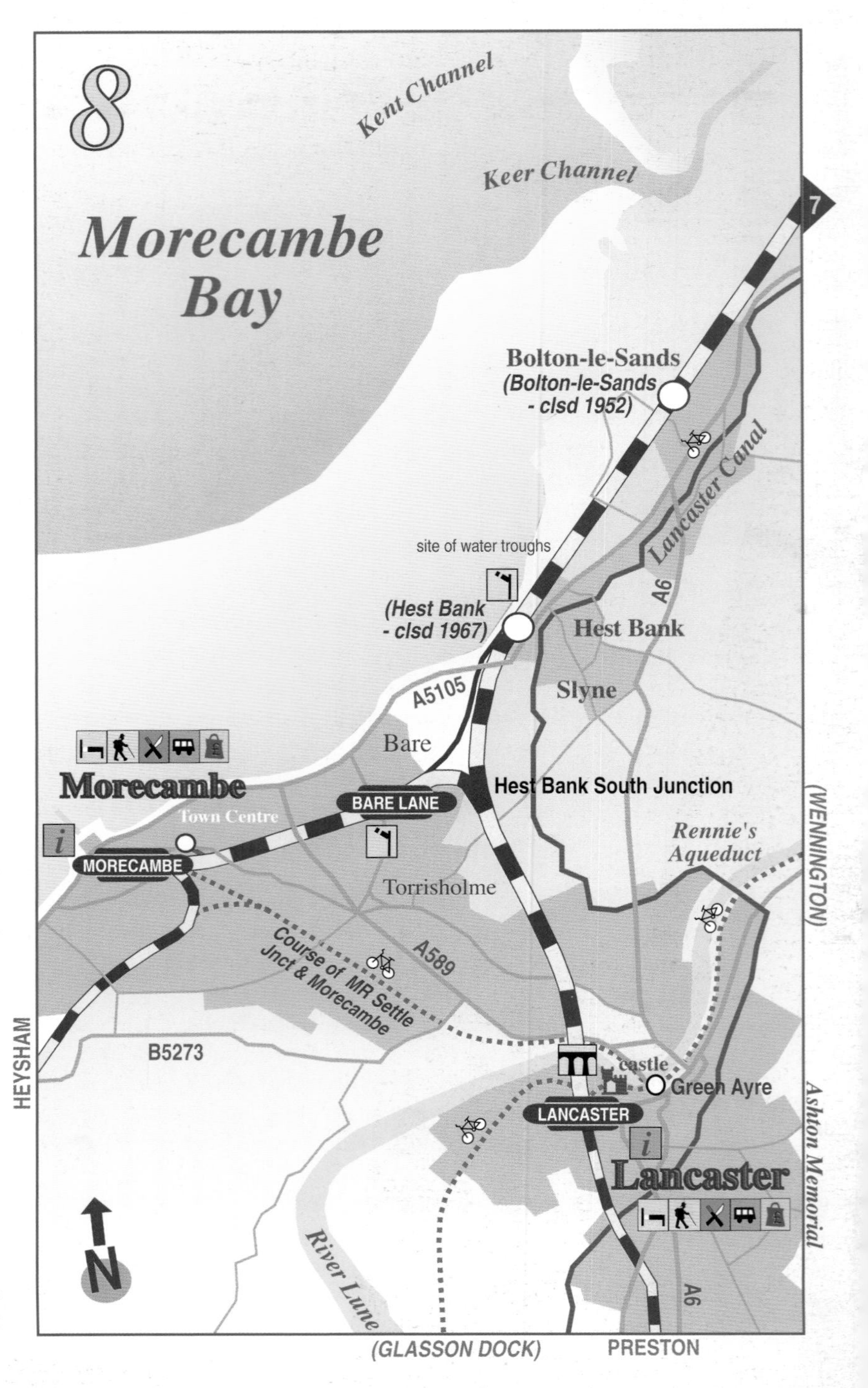

SETTLE APPLEBY CARLISLE

Settle

Dent

Ais Gill

Kirkby Stephen

EMERGING from a rocky cutting of some depth, the train approaches SETTLE station, 510 feet above sea level. To the east limestone outcrops rear up in a geological firework display of crags and caves and waterfalls. It is difficult to maintain an English stiff upper lip; to not break out in spontaneous applause like some Japanese tour group.

Settle sets the architectural tone for all the stations between here and Carlisle. The style has been labelled 'Derby Gothic', a reference to the Midland Railway's headquarters and design centre. S&C stations were built to a common style in three sizes. Settle, along with the other market towns of Kirkby Stephen and Appleby, is of the largest size. Though the specification was common, the materials used were local: limestone and millstone grit between Settle and Kirkby Stephen, brick at Appleby, and sandstone through the Eden Valley. The stone used at Settle is said to have been quarried near Bradford. Perhaps the most unusual feature of the station buildings is that access to them can only be made from the platform side and not, as in most cases elsewhere, from the roadway as well. Probably it was just a case of minimising draughts in such windswept climes.

Look out for the ornamental bargeboards decorating the gable ends, and the elegant screen fronting the entrance to the booking hall. The Friends of the Settle & Carlisle operate a souvenir shop in one of the rooms adjoining the booking hall, and they have also refurbished the signal cabin, though it is no longer in operational use, and has been moved slightly to the north of its original position so as to facilitate visitor access.

In the cosy, well-appointed booking hall a replica nameplate commemorates the naming of an LMS Patriot Class locomotive after the nearby public school, Giggleswick. The ceremony took place on 4th November 1938, though the locomotive had been built five years earlier. The two youngest boys in the school, then aged eight, unveiled the nameplate. When *Giggleswick* was withdrawn in 1962 the school was presented with one of the pair of nameplates. More recently they auctioned it to fund school improvements and were probably amazed when it realised a value of £16,300! The railway writer, O.S. Nock, was educated at Giggleswick and the late television personality, Russell Harty, taught there at one time.

The footbridge looks as though it has always been there, but dates from as recently as 1993, having been brought in,

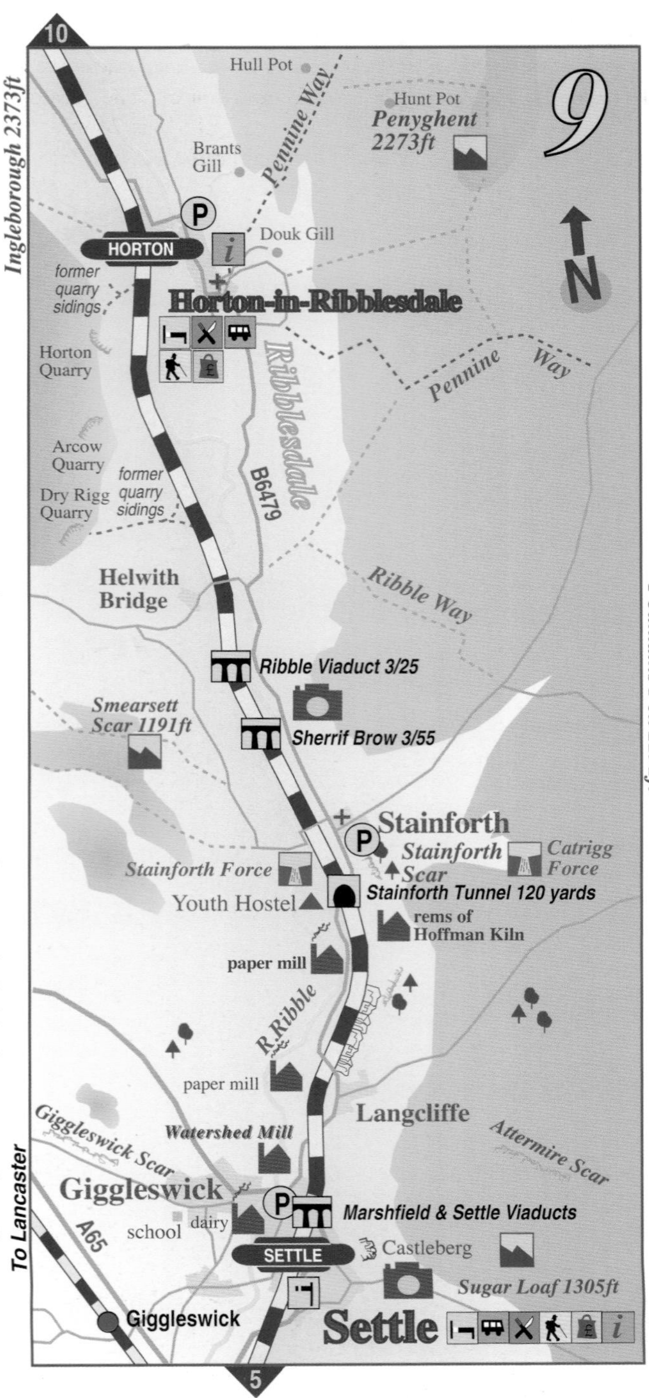

decidedly secondhand, from Drem near Edinburgh to cope with increasing levels of tourism never previously experienced in this quiet market town. In contrast with the main station buildings on the 'up' platform, the 'down' (northbound) platform is graced only by a simple waiting room. Beyond the boundary wall, part stone, part Midland diagonal fencing, the land drops away into the valley of the Ribble then climbs again towards the neighbouring community of Giggleswick, dominated by the domed chapel of the school. In the foreground, hiding the river, stands the local creamery together with a former mill now used for storage by a paper making company.

After a brief respite through the station, the line resumes its 1 in 100 climb and crosses a pair of viaducts. The railway is already considerably higher than the river which, between Settle and Langcliffe, has attracted a sudden flurry of mills. One of these, Watershed Mill, has been redeveloped to house a number of speciality shops, two others are still in the business of paper making.

Though the Midland's primary motive for building the Settle & Carlisle was for the Scottish traffic, a welcome revenue-earning by-product was the development of several large lineside quarries. The first of these was opened by the Craven Lime Company at Stainforth in 1873. Its most notable feature was the massive 'Hoffman' limestone burning kiln topped by a 200ft high chimney. Engine drivers would reputedly draw this chimney to the attention of young and gullible firemen, pointing out that their train had to reach that height before it got to Ribblehead, so they'd better knuckle down and fill the firebox with coal. The former quarry is backed by Stainforth Scar, a dramatic rockface popular with local climbers.

At STAINFORTH the Ribble Valley narrows to almost gorge-like dimensions, and the S&C encounters its first, albeit brief, tunnel. To pass through this gorge at its narrowest point the railway builders had to divert the river, which is crossed twice in only a few hundred yards. The B6479 shares the valley with the railway. A constant stream of quarry lorries uses the road carrying stone from the Horton area. One doesn't have to be a railway fan to wish that this traffic went by rail to the general benefit of the environment. But lorry driving is a significant facet of the local economy and it is questionable whether the National Park authority have the commitment, let alone the clout, to have the stone transferred to rail.

HORTON station once won the area's Best Kept station

competition for seventeen years on the trot. Though unstaffed now, of course, it retains a well-kept air, having recently been refurbished and let out as offices. Behind the station looms the leonine summit of Penyghent, 2,273ft above sea level and crossed by the Pennine Way. It's one of a trio of famous peaks which dominate this part of the Yorkshire Dales. The other two are Ingleborough and Whernside. Ingleborough stands about three miles to the west of the line, slightly to the north of Penyghent and has a distinctively flat top to it.

Both mountains, and indeed Whernside as well, can be reached on foot from Horton station. The greatest challenge is to visit all the Three Peaks in a day. The round trip is 24 miles long and can be done, if you're fit, in around a dozen hours. The best fell runners in the annual Three Peaks Race manage it in two and a half hours!

Non-stop through Horton - Arriva's celebrated 'top & tail' train races southwards through Horton-in-Ribblesdale

Sunset over Ribblhead - a steam charter catches the last rays of the dying sun as it makes its way across Batty Moss and on to Blea Moor

Bob Green

IF there is much enjoyment to be had on the surface of Three Peaks country, another sort of pleasure entirely can be derived from exploration of the underground world of caves and potholes which riddle this limestone landscape. Potholing - it goes without saying - is an activity for the experienced, but even the average rambler can gain a sense of the excitement involved by visiting some of the more spectacular 'pots' which form the entrance points to this subterranean world. Alum Pot, above the hamlet of Selside, is one of the better known ones well worth going to see. The water which disappears into Alum Pot flows down off Simon Fell, then emerges beside the Ribble at Tarn Dub, east of the railway.

The line climbs two hundred feet in five miles as the landscape redoubles its sense of remoteness. Dwellings become few and far between, and you sense that the people who do live here have to be as hardy as the sheep which graze the drystone wall encompassed pastures. Most of this walling dates from the 18th century. Prior to that, Ribblesdale would have been an even more intimidating wilderness. Beneath the flanks of Simon Fell and Park Fell, SELSIDE huddles under the railway embankment. The Midland Railway built two rows of employees cottages here which are still inhabited. They would have provided homes for local signalmen and permanent way staff. Architecturally they echo the style of station buildings along the line - Derby Gothic takes on the moorland wastes!

Alas the eccentric anomaly whereby RIBBLEHEAD station was for several years only served by southbound trains came to an end in 1993 when the down platform was reinstated. The new platform boasts a pretty little stone shelter in a parody of Midland style, and any regret evinced by connoisseurs of bizarre railway operation must be outweighed by the welcome opening up of Ribblehead, and its moorland fastness, to railbourne visitors again. The station itself has been restored and opens its doors to the general public as a small visitor centre with exhibitions devoted to the story of the Settle & Carlisle line's construction and operation.

Save for the welcoming pub at the foot of the station drive, signs of civilisation are conspicuously absent, a state of affairs which leads you to reflect that the station made an admirable choice as a weather station, a status conferred upon it in 1938. Stationmasters here received special training in the arts of wind

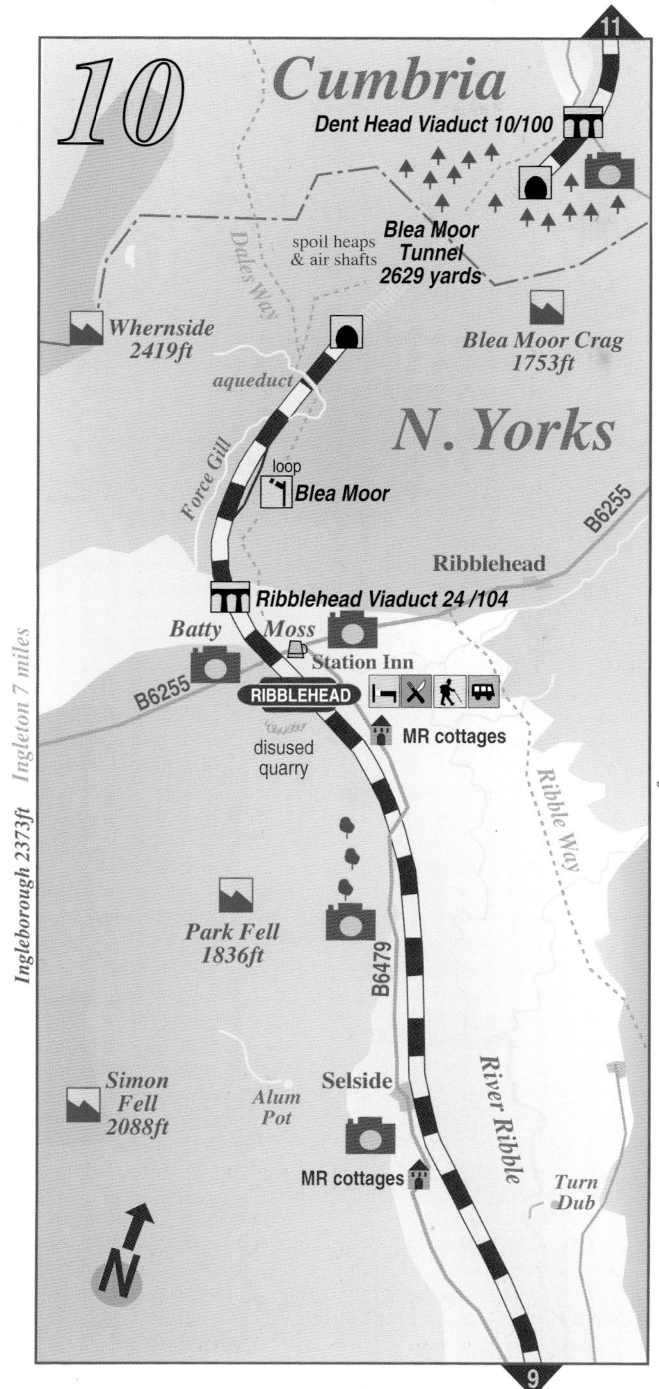

speed calibration and rainfall calculation, after all they probably had more inches of rain to count than tickets to sell.

Ribblehead Viaduct is the Settle & Carlisle's most potent and famous image. It spreads twenty-four colossal arches across the shakehole-strewn bog of Batty Moss, a name that in earlier days it bore. Statistics are superfluous in the presence of such grandeur, but for those who care for such data the viaduct is a quarter of a mile long and over a hundred feet high. In the 1980s it became the crux of British Rail's argument that the line would have to close. Cost cutting by the original 19th century contractors led to deterioration in the structure which British Rail, anxious to find good cause to close the Settle & Carlisle, were only too happy to present to the public and politicians alike as beyond economically viable repair. Wildcat figures amounting to several millions of pounds were bandied about like stock market flotations. In the event the viaduct underwent repair at significantly less cost.

Batty Moss gives way to Blea Moor, the almost poetic resonance of such names matched only by the grandeur of the wild landscape. The signalmen at BLEA MOOR box are as lonely as lighthouse keepers. Their box controls access to and from the single track section over Ribblehead Viaduct, together with a loop where southbound goods trains can be stored to let passenger trains overtake them.

Overlooked by the eastern flank of Whernside, most northerly of the Three Peaks, the line delves into cuttings, passing under an unusual aqueduct carrying Force Gill and the Dales Way, before penetrating the southern portal of Blea Moor Tunnel. This took five years to dig. Seven shafts were sunk from the moor above, the extracted rock being winched up and deposited in spoil mounds on the inhospitable moor. Three of the shafts were retained for ventilation, whilst the spoil, grassed over now, remains like a series of malignant growths on the swarthy surface of the moor.

The moorland above the northern portal of Blea Moor has been planted, somewhat contentiously, with conifers. Traditionalists loathe the changed aspect brought to the once bare fells by such plantations, but those of us who come up here from a muted world of motorways and housing estates tend to be grateful for any hue and texture of green. Dashing out of the darkness of the tunnel the railway finds itself at the head of Dentdale. DENT HEAD VIADUCT is one of the most photographed on the line.

PASSENGERS on the western side of the train are treated to an incomparable prospect of Dentdale, now part of Cumbria but once, more appropriately, in Yorkshire's West Riding. Far below, the River Dee skips down the valley over a succession of limestone steps, beneath which it is apt to disappear after prolonged spells of dry weather. It is accompanied by a by-road which also forms the course of the Dales Way, an 84 mile long distance path leading from Ilkley to Windermere. The hamlet of Stone House was once the site of a marble quarry. ARTEN GILL VIADUCT was built from this peculiarly coloured local rock, a darkish grey limestone streaked with the patterns of white fossils. Arten Gill Viaduct is arguably the Settle & Carlisle's most dramatic in terms of its setting high on the shoulders of Dent Fell.

DENT occupies a niche in railway record books for, at 1150ft above sea level, it was always feted as the highest station on a main line in England. It is five miles horizontally and six hundred feet vertically from the village it purports to serve; though, to the sturdy inhabitants of Dentdale, well used to ascending onto the fell to dig for coal, this was obviously all in a day's work. The stationmaster's house was said to have been the first in England to be double-glazed. Its walls were also slated for added protection against the elements on three sides. Snow fences above the railway cutting emphasise the Wagnerian character of the weather. These days they are grotesquely eroded and remind you of a derelict groyne on an exposed beach. The station building has been converted into a private residence. Substantial shelters on both platforms provide welcome retreats after a hard day's hoofing on the fells. The strange little building to the south of the station is thought to have been an original navvies bothy.

RISE HILL TUNNEL, second only to Blea Moor in terms of length, ushers the northbound train from Dentdale to Garsdale, a valley watered by the River Clough, a tributary of the Lancaster Lune. Garsdale's best known settlement is Sedbergh, famous for its public school. In steam days, water troughs were fitted between the rails between Rise Hill and Garsdale to enable express trains to pick up water without needing to stop. Nowadays steam excursionists greet the water stop at Garsdale as a good excuse to stretch their legs.

GARSDALE is a sort of Hellifield in miniature. Here in the middle of nowhere stood a railway community whose purpose is heavily hinted at by the station's original name of "Hawes Junction." The single track branch line to the Wensleydale

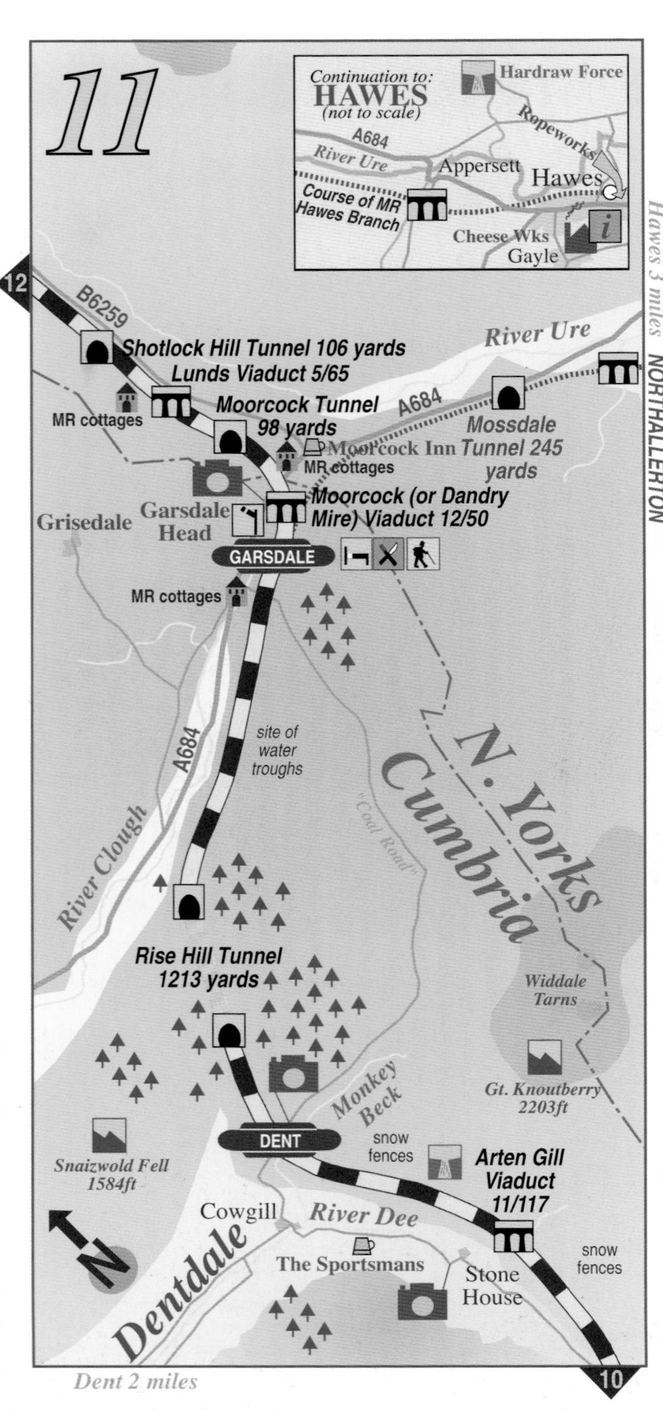

market town of Hawes was six miles long and trains took around a dozen minutes to reach the typically S&C styled station there, before proceeding along North Eastern Railway tracks to Northallerton. By all accounts it was a journey of spellbinding loveliness which the Wensleydale Railway Association are actively reviving, and already trains have been reinstated on an eleven mile section between Leyburn and Leeming Bar.

It may not have been much of a population centre, but as far as the Midland Railway was concerned, Garsdale was the most significant station between Settle and Carlisle. It had been intended that a locomotive depot be provided here, but in the event facilities were limited to a water crane and turntable. The turntable entered railway folklore one tempestuous night when a searing wind caught a locomotive being turned and span it round and round and round until someone had the presence of mind to pour sand on the moving parts, bringing the whole contraption to a shuddering halt. To avoid being similarly embarrassed again a pallisade of old railway sleepers was built up around the turntable to act as a windbreak. The deck from Garsdale turntable has found a new lease of life at Keighley on the Worth Valley Railway.

Sixteen company houses were built for the staff at Garsdale. It was a tight-knit community, living like Hebridean islanders surrounded by a sea of unremitting moorland. Their pleasures were simple. The water tank doubled as a dance hall and cinema, church services were held in one of the waiting rooms, and in another room there was a staff library. Old photographs reveal how pretty the station looked. An extended canopy sheltered the 'island' platform at whose outer face the Wensleydale trains stood patiently waiting for the next connection from the main line.

Pulling away from Garsdale the train passes a disconsolate rank of rusty sidings - there are no wagons to shunt for Wensleydale now - and crosses MOORCOCK VIADUCT which carries the line across a boggy area known as Dandry Mire. The engineers had planned to build an embankment across the mire, but all the earth they tipped just sank into the bog. They tipped and tipped for two years of Victorian obstinacy before abandoning the embankment and building this fine viaduct instead. On the roadside to the west, where the railway crosses the Sedbergh-Hawes road, stands the tiny Hawes Junction Methodist Chapel. Dales folk, in common with others whose lives were led at the sharp end of existence, were devoutly chapel as opposed to church. Tunnels and viaducts follow in quick succession as the line heads towards its summit at Ais Gill.

Robert Armitstead

Empties for Ayrshire - a Freightliner coal train makes its way through Dent on its way to the port of Hunterston on the Clyde to collect another load of imported coal

A southbound Green Express charter crosses Ais Gill Viaduct hauled by Fragonset Class 47 47701 *Waverley*

Robert Armitstead

AIS GILL is one of the great British railway summits. Its name belongs in the same hall of fame as Shap, Beattock, Talerdigg, Dainton and Druimuachdar. Here, twenty-three miles from Settle and forty-nine from Carlisle, the line has reached the ridge tiles of its climb, 1169ft above sea level. It can be a turbulent, desolate place, overlooked by Wild Boar Fell on one side and the watershed of the Ure and Eden rivers on the other. The Midland Railway provided sidings at the summit for slow trains to be stored or banking engines detached. Ais Gill signal box has been removed and is now preserved at the Midland Railway Centre in Derbyshire, but the employees cottages remain in domestic use. From the eastern side of the train you might catch a glimpse of Hell Gill waterfall; strange that the source of Eden should be known as Hell.

Tucked under the hem of Little Fell, the line descends at the ruling gradient of 1 in 100 with a brief easing at the site of Mallerstang sidings. Westwards, views from the carriage windows are restricted to outcrops of moss covered rock, waterfalls and the occasional precipitous pasture wrought tenaciously out of the fellside. Eastwards the scene is splendidly reminiscent of that offered by the best Alpine railways. The Eden, encouraged by the support of numerous becks and gills, pursues a northbound course along the valley floor. Lonely whitewashed farmhouses stand sequestered at the end of steep, rutted tracks. The world does not beat a path to such doors. Post vans, mobile grocers, and animal feeds reps are possibly the only regular visitors to farmyards where a marked degree of rural poverty exists beyond the ken of Whitehall's statisticians.

The only community of any sort is the hamlet of Outhgill whose chapel can be seen beside the river. It has associations with Lady Anne Clifford, an indomitable 17th century gentlewoman still venerated in the Dales and the Eden Valley. She was born at Skipton Castle in 1590 into a family of aristocrats who later moved to London where she was brought up on the peripheries of the Royal court. In 1605 her wealthy father died but she was disinherited by his brother and nephew. She spent the next thirty years campaigning to regain her inheritance, but it was not until the death of her cousin that her father's estate reverted to her. In the interim the family's estates in the north of England had been allowed to fall into rack and ruin and Lady Anne set about reviving them. To reach Outhgill she travelled along the old green road which follows the

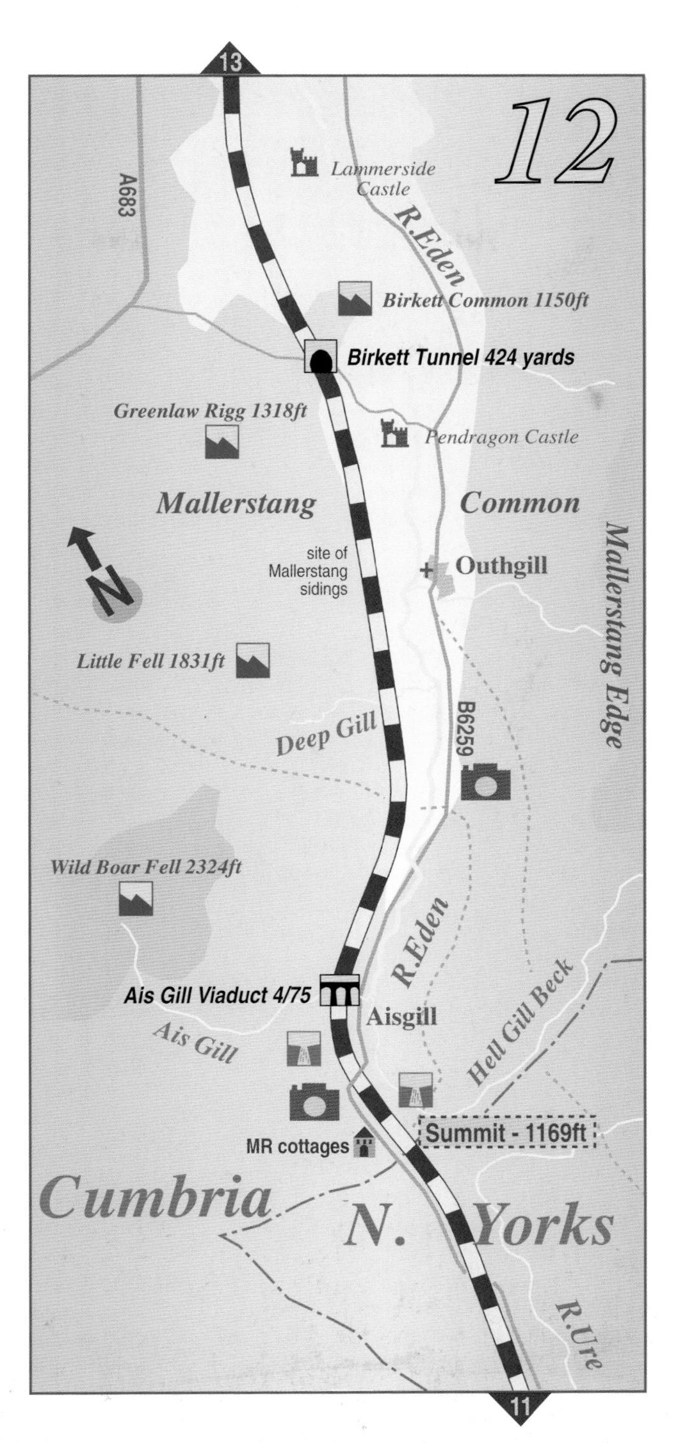

escarpment. In her diary for 1663 she wrote of going "over Cotter in my coach - where I think a coach never went before - and over Helgill Bridge into Westmorland." She went on to restore Pendragon, Brough and Appleby castles and was buried in St Lawrence's, Appleby in 1676.

For a number of years now the Railway Heritage Trust has been making grants towards restoration of the dry-stone boundary walls which accompany the Settle & Carlisle line. Local dry-stone wallers have been subcontracted to undertake this painstaking work and on a number of occasions helicopters have been employed to air-lift in the stones required to remote stretches of the railway not easily accessed by road. In 2002 the sympathetic nature of this work was recognised by the winning of a National Railway Heritage Award.

A widening of the trackbed level with Outhgill marks the site of Mallerstang sidings. The Midland Railway had an aversion for 'facing points' on main lines. And so instead of providing loops which a train could enter at one end and leave at the other, they preferred to let their goods trains reverse into a siding when the need arose for them to be overtaken by an express or when entering a goods yard. As built the only facing point between Settle and the outskirts of Carlisle was at Appleby where a branch from the down main line linked up with the North Eastern Railway. In the 'up' direction there were no facing points at all until loops were laid at Blea Moor during the Second World War. Mallerstang sidings were taken out of use in 1969.

Legend has it that Pendragon Castle was once the home of King Arthur's father, Uther Pendragon. It makes a nice story, but logic suggests that the building is more likely to have originated as a tower of defence against Scottish attacks in the 12th century. Lady Anne Clifford spent Christmas 1663 here and wrote of watching the moon over Wild Boar Fell and listening to the Eden gurgling over its bed.

Views of Pendragon are swallowed up by the deep cutting which forms the approach to Birkett Tunnel. Whilst you are inside the tunnel nature effects a quick scene change and, on emerging from the northern portal, you sense that the mountainous country - familiar since Horton-in-Ribblesdale - is being left behind. From the eastern side of the train you can enjoy a last lingering view of the youthful Eden picking its way around the foot of Birkett Common under the receding headlands of High Pike Hill, Tailbridge Hill and Nine Standards Rigg; the last with its nine cairns clearly countable if visibility is good.

KIRKBY STEPHEN 'West', as it was once known to differentiate it from the North Eastern Railway's 'East' station, emphasises that the Midland's priority was to reach Scotland, and that serving of any communities encountered on the way was of secondary consideration. The station is almost two miles out of town and a hundred and fifty feet higher, perched like a social outcast on the edge of the moors. Had the line been built any lower for the benefit of Kirkby Stephen, the southbound climb to Ais Gill would have been correspondingly much steeper. In any case, the North Eastern was already catering for Kirkby Stephen's local traffic, the lines to Tebay, Penrith and Barnard Castle having opened independently in 1861. It also bears remembering that, in the days before the motor car, people were accustomed to walking much further. Today we baulk at having to leave the car at the far end of the supermarket car park. In Victorian times country folk thought nothing of walking several miles to work or shop or school.

The Midland station at KIRKBY STEPHEN was built to the same specification as Settle and Appleby. It has recently been refurbished to good effect, though no firm proposals as to its new use had been arrived at as we went to press. The footbridge is also a new addition - saving what had always been a long walk round by the road - as is the neat stone-built waiting room on the down side. A large goods shed was provided together with a cattle dock capable of handling up to ten wagons at a time. Goods trains stopped calling at the yard in 1964 and these days it's used, ironically, by a road transport haulier called Sam Ostle whose fleet of smart tanker vehicles have evocative names prefixed with 'Eden' in the manner of the 'Western' diesel hydraulic locomotives.

The busy main road from Kendal to Brough passes beneath the railway and is lined on one side by former railway worker's cottages. The signal box, a replacement structure of 1950s vintage, remains in use, and if the train is late you can telephone the signalman and ask - politely! - for an explanation.

The mountains may be behind you now, but the Settle & Carlisle's tallest viaduct is just around the corner. With the four rounded towers of Smardale Hall in view to the east, the railway crosses SMARDALE VIADUCT, a gracefully curving structure built from grey limestone. It's popular with photographers, though they face a stiffish walk to get the best views. The delightfully named Scandal Beck runs beneath

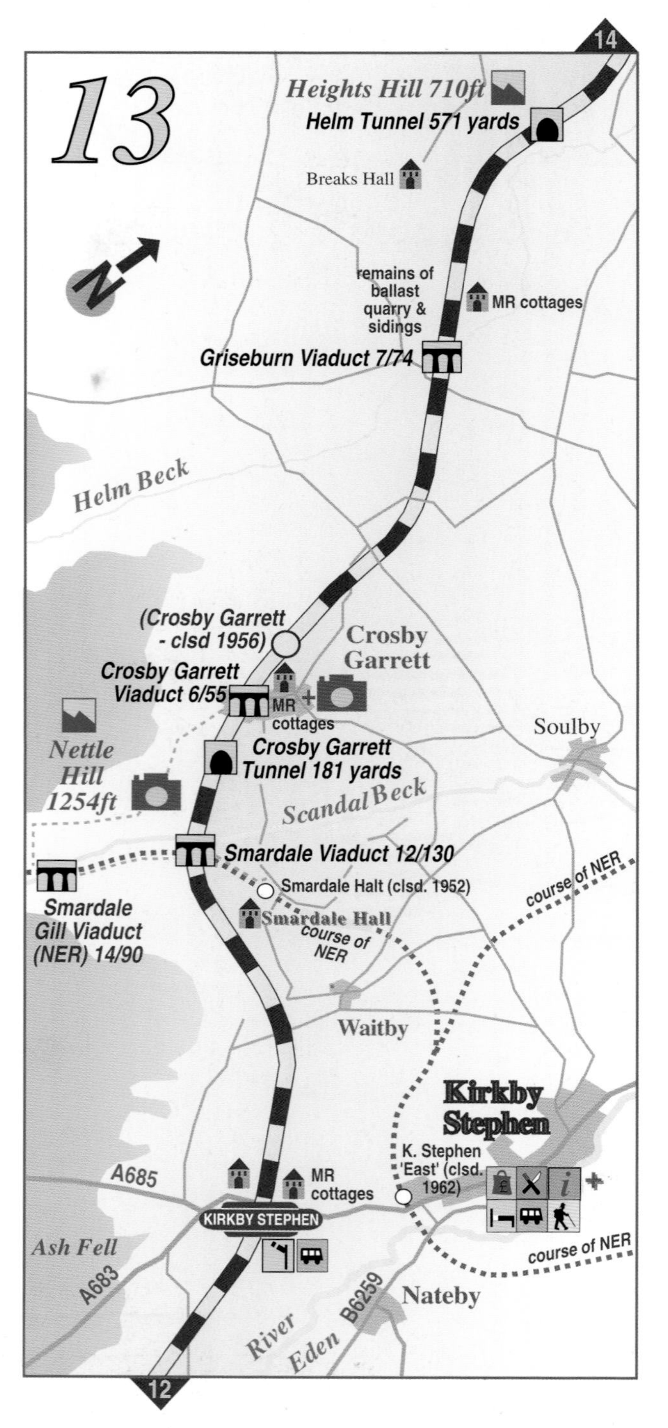

Smardale Viaduct, trickling down from Ravenstonedale to find the Eden. Many railway enthusiasts consider the closure of the Tebay-Barnard Castle route over Stainmore to have been a scandal too. It shut in 1962 amidst much controversy. British Railways had cooked the books and even turned down the offer of a local quarry owner, who made much use of the line, to buy it outright and operate it privately. The line's most famous structure was the 196ft high cast iron girder viaduct at Belah, a national monument if ever there was one, cynically demolished in 1963, but another notable viaduct still stands at Smardale and is momentarily visible from the west side of the train. It can still be crossed, albeit on foot, as part of the trackbed has been incorporated by the Cumbria Wildlife Trust into a permissive path for the public. These hillsides were the site of Romano-British settlements and also contain the intriguing remnants of Medieval man-made rabbit warrens, created to provide food for the inhabitants.

A short tunnel and another viaduct precede the site of CROSBY GARRETT station, closed in 1956. The station platforms occupied a cutting and you can still glimpse the indentations left behind. A sizeable cattle dock was provided in the goods yard for this prosperous agricultural area. From the viaduct the village looks gorgeous and vice versa. A beck runs between a haphazard street plan of stone built houses. The church stands aloof on an artificial mound reckoned to have been the site of an Iron Age temple. Locals prefer the story that the devil made the mound to deter the old and infirm from seeking the solace of their maker. Nowadays the village is more infamous for being bereft of a pub.

It is difficult to accept that GRISEBURN VIADUCT marks the half-way point between Settle and Carlisle. Subconsciously one expects the middle to be somewhere up in the mountains. But, in reality, the route climbs abruptly from Settle to Ais Gill before falling more gently towards Carlisle. Ian Nairn, the late great architectural and travel writer and broadcaster, with typical eloquence, referred to the section north of Ais Gill as the line's "long diminuendo", and that sums it up very well. Griseburn Viaduct carries the line across Helm Beck, a tributary of the Eden. North of the viaduct the Midland had a ballast quarry, the remains of which are to be seen on the western side of the track. It took three years to dig the relatively short HELM TUNNEL through the red marl of Heights Hill. The date of its completion, 1873, is embossed in stone above each portal.

Peter J. Robinson

Coal empties for Carlisle - an EWS Class 66 hauls high capacity coal wagons past Waitby, typifying the Settle & Carlisle's present-day role as a trunk route for heavy freight

Appleby's station looks warm and welcoming on a wet winter evening

GREAT ORMSIDE is another abandoned station, closed in 1952. One registers the blurred shapes of the now familiar 'Derby Gothic' buildings. Rarely can a railway have exhibited such homogeneity in its accoutrements. Most main lines were built piecemeal by independent companies at the outset of the Railway Age. Travel from Euston or Kings Cross to Glasgow and you pass over the tracks of several constituents. Even the Great Western's line from London to the West Country displays a remarkable diversity in architectural styles. Only on the now closed Great Central Railway from Marylebone to the East Midlands and South Yorkshire was such a prevailing pattern of building styles and station design so obvious.

North of Great Ormside the railway crosses the River Eden for the first of two times. The river has grown in stature since last seen back at Birkett Common. After passing under the line it curves gracefully towards Appleby around the base of a wooded hill and accompanied by a riparian footpath. To the east the high fells return, stretching up towards the Lune Forest, a sponge-like wilderness of watershed country familiar only to walkers on the Pennine Way and soldiers out on target practice.

From the western side of the train the turreted Norman tower of Appleby Castle comes into view. It resembles one of those simple model forts children played with before the advent of computer games. By all accounts, however, it stood like a red rag to the bull-like tendencies of the Scots who repeatedly sacked the town throughout the Middle Ages, the worst occasion being in 1388, from which, some say, Appleby has never really recovered. As the train slows down for the Appleby stop it passes a former dairy from which a special train of milk tankers was despatched daily to Cricklewood so that Londoners could savour the creamy taste of milk produced by the Eden Valley's contented cows. In our lorry-based economy it's easy to forget how important the railways once were for the carriage of all manner of goods, but happily there are signs of a resurgence in rail freight, and it's not wholly impossible that locally produced commodities such as milk, timber and aggregates might once again be carried along the Settle & Carlisle corridor.

APPLEBY'S long platforms were built for Anglo-Scottish expresses and 'Sprinters' look lost in them. Only the occasional charter train does them justice now, and Appleby can suddenly resemble Paddington at peak hour when five hundred excursionists spill off their train to photograph their locomotive

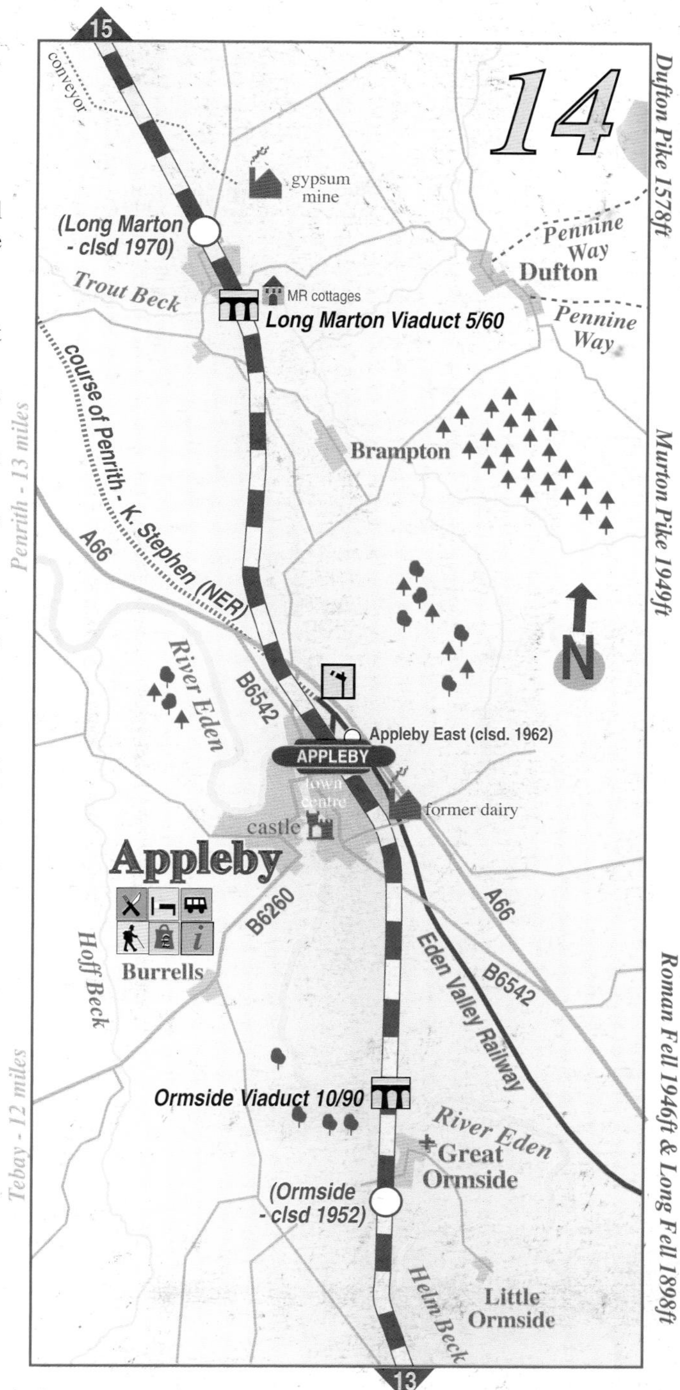

taking water or patronise FoSCL's souvenir shop. The water tank and crane were rebuilt by the local Round Table in 1991. The classic S&C goods shed is another revitalised structure, enjoying a new lease of life as the Appleby Heritage Centre.

In a perfect world all small town stations would be as attractive, as cosy and as welcoming as Appleby, which won the Best Kept Small Station Award in 2003. Have you noticed that the buildings are of brick not stone? In winter a stove glows in the waiting room which is liberally strewn with tourist material and interpretive information. On the side of the station building a plaque commemorates Eric Treacy, a bishop and one of the great railway photographers, who collapsed and died on Appleby station whilst photographing a steam special. He was of the view that the Settle & Carlisle, York Minster and Hadrian's Wall constituted the three chief man-made wonders of northern England, apparently absent-mindedly omitting to mention the fourth - Farrah's Original Harrogate Toffee.

Appleby has another station to which fate, so far at any rate, hasn't been so magnanimous. Appleby East was served by the Kirkby Stephen-Penrith line of the North Eastern Railway which we first encountered earlier in the journey. Losing its passenger services in 1962, goods traffic miraculously survived for another twenty-seven years, in the final years being confined to military traffic to and from the firing ranges at Warcop. These six miles of track remain in situ and have recently been given to Sustrans for conversion into a cycleway. It may well also provide a springboard for the ambitions of the Eden Valley Railway Company who, ultimately, would like to relay the line back to Kirkby Stephen East, and perhaps in a pipe dream even beyond to a rebuilt Belah Viaduct.

The northbound train pulls away from Appleby on a high embankment, escaping into a pleasant landscape of farmland spread about the Eden Valley. To the east, in the foothills of the fells, stand a trio of conical summits known locally, after the Lakeland fashion, as pikes. Murton Pike, Dufton Pike and Knock Pike can easily be picked out from the train in normal weather conditions.

LONG MARTON viaduct was built from stone quarried at Dufton. Six railway employees cottages nestle under the eastern side of the adjoining embankment. Closed as recently as 1970, the station retains its buildings and its goods shed. An aerial ropeway once brought barytes down from a mine high on the slopes of Great Dun Fell.

CROSS FELL, the highest point in the Pennines, steals the show as the northbound train skips downhill through the aptly named Eden Valley. The railway has dropped out of the higher hills - the former station at Newbiggin stands 400ft above sea level - but on the eastern side of the line the Pennine chain continues its muscular domination of the landscape. The broad summit of Cross Fell is said to bear snow for three-quarters of the calendar. Legend has it that St Augustine named it after building a cross on its summit to ward off evil spirits. But any spectre prepared to haunt its heathery tops must be a hardy soul indeed. Ask anyone who has toiled to its top whilst tackling the "Pennine Way", or huddled behind the stone-built shelter on its summit, taking refuge from the Helm Wind, a violent north-easterly prevalent in late winter and early spring. Mike Cudahy, the fell runner and first man to complete the 270 miles of the "Pennine Way" in under three days, wrote of Cross Fell as being "magnificent, but not trustworthy" and "not beautiful, but commanding of respect." The River Tees rises on Cross Fell's sinewy south-western shoulder before striding through Yorkshire and Cleveland to pour itself into the North Sea. Yet just a few clumps of bog grass away lies the source of Crowdundle Beck, which elects to flow westwards down over the screes of Wildboar Scar and pass under the railway to join the Eden.

If Cross Fell is unquestionably the star in this part of the Pennines, it has a strong supporting cast. To the south lies Great Dun Fell, unmistakably topped by the Civil Aviation Authority's radar station, whilst on the skirts of the fells stand some peculiar cultivation terraces mysteriously known as the Hanging Walls of Mark Anthony.

Gypsum mining has flourished hereabouts for a couple of centuries. The works at Kirkby Thore is operated by British Gypsum who use rail to bring gypsum in from Drax Power Station in Yorkshire, where it is a by-product of the de-sulphurisation process. Gypsum is also extracted from three local drift mines and a surface quarry. A conveyor belt links the various sites with the main works where it is crushed, ground, heated and added to chemicals to produce raw plaster.

The Midland Railway spelt NEW BIGGIN as two words, the Ordnance Survey gives it one. The station building, station-master's house and a quartet of employees cottages remain intact and in use as private dwellings. The station building is of the smallest S&C type and built from a fresh, creamy-coloured stone

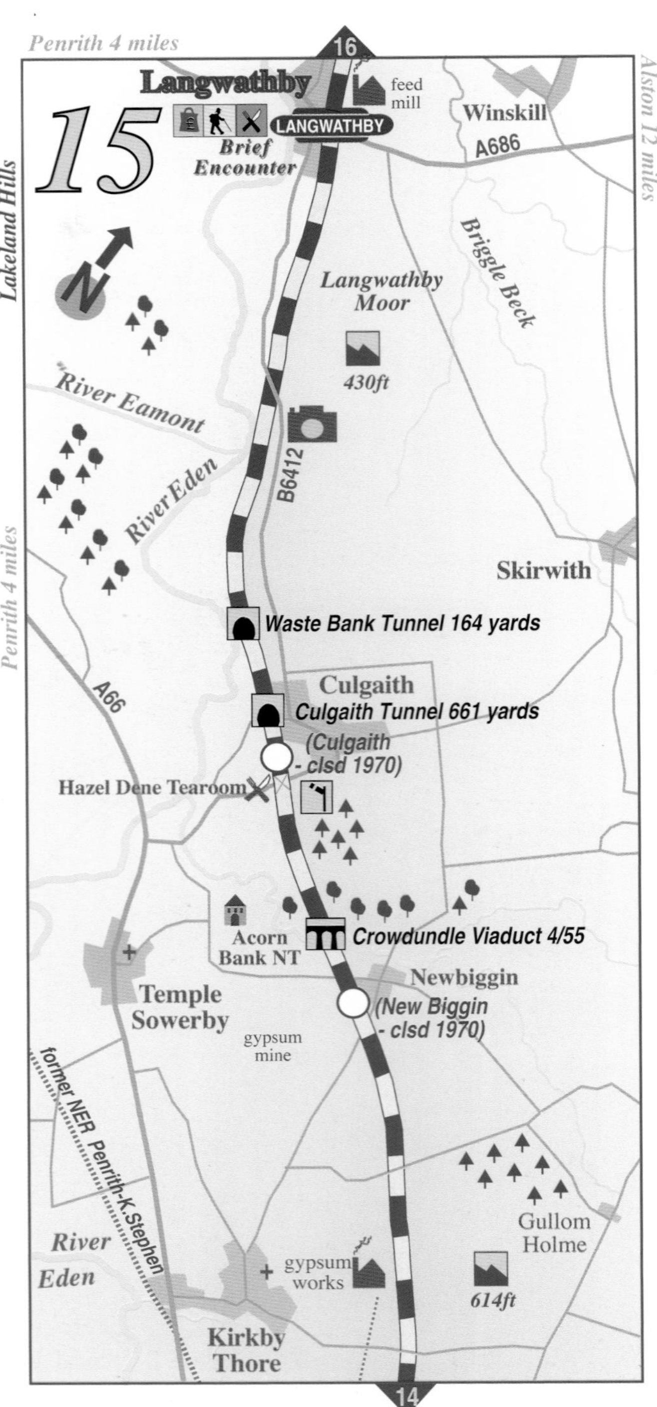

with sandstone trimmings. To the north of the station a viaduct carries the line over Crowdundle Beck, formerly the boundary between the old counties of Westmorland and Cumberland. From the western side of the train there is a tantalising glimpse of the National Trust property of Acorn Bank whose aromatic herb garden is open to the public.

Envious stares may be emanating from those seated on the western side of the train as they crane their necks to pick out the salient features of the Pennine backbone, but they have their own mountain range - if a more distant one - to enjoy, not to mention the gorgeous Eden itself as it comes back into view beyond the two short tunnels at Culgaith. The Lakeland summits are too distant, and the train too swift, to be anything other than a blur, though Helvellyn's jagged outline is unmistakable.

The Midland didn't intend to have a station at CULGAITH until they had their corporate arm twisted by the local vicar. One imagines their engineer complying with the cleric's demands over a glass or two of good port. In the event Culgaith station opened four years after the rest of the line, its most peculiar aspect being its architectural style, quite unlike the off the shelf buildings along the rest of the line. Built from local stone, the single storey structure, with its steeply pitched roof, looks more like the lodge house to a country seat. Nowadays it, and the adjacent crossing-keeper's house, are private homes, though the signal box remains in use, guarding the level crossing. On the opposite side of the line a garden centre incorporates a tea room decorated with some interesting railway memorabilia.

Between Culgaith and Lazonby the River Eamont makes an entrance, its confluence with the Eden occurring amidst broad meadows which provide a fertile wintering ground for wild geese. The Eamont has its origins in the Lake District, flowing out of Ullswater, and down past Penrith, where it is joined by the Lowther, which runs off the northern flank of Shap Fell. The canoeist, William Bliss, wrote endearingly of the Eamont and Eden in his book *Rapid Rivers*, published in 1935. He describes a Whitsuntide night camping here with his Canadian canoe and a dip at dawn followed by a breakfast of freshly caught trout. Ah, those were the days!

LANGWATHBY station building houses a pleasant cafe called "Brief Encounter". This is an appropriate use of a station now that most of them aren't staffed anymore. The old goods shed has been incorporated into the extensive premises of a poultry products firm rejoicing in the name of Frank Bird.

A southbound steam charter climbs through New Biggin behind a pristine Stanier 'Pacific' 46203 *Princess Margaret Rose*

Bob Green

Classic traction, classic scenery - a double-headed Class 50 charter negotiates the Eden Gorge near Lazonby

Peter J. Robinson

IT is unfortunate that LITTLE SALKELD station has not re-opened since its closure in 1970, for it would be useful for visitors to two local attractions: the working water mill and Long Meg's stone circle. The railway crosses the Eden for only the second time by way of Eden Lacy Viaduct; four of the bridge's six piers being permanently washed by the northward flow of the river, an indication of its growing breadth since it was previously crossed by the line at Ormside, south of Appleby.

Downstream of the viaduct the river foams across a weir at the site of a former mill. In medieval times there was a pack-horse bridge here as well. Immediately south of the viaduct lies the once extensive Long Meg mineral sidings. A pair of rusty loops remain intact, presided over by a 'locked out' signal box. Silver birch and rosebay willowherb, those eager colonisers of wastegrounds, flourish where lines of wagons once waited to be loaded with anhydrite, a source of sulphur shipped in considerable tonnages to an ICI chemical works at Widnes, near Liverpool.

Round a bend in the river stand Lacy's Caves, a series of chambers hewn out of the soft sandstone, said to have been the work of Colonel Samuel Lacy who lived at Salkeld Hall in the 18th century. One story suggests that the colonel employed a man to live in the caves as a hermit in order to add an aura of romantic dissolution to the neighbourhood. One gets a Pythonesque picture of a job centre offering positions for well paid hermits today - please form an orderly queue.

South of Lazonby's short tunnel stood a set of sidings serving a railway owned sand pit. The sand extracted here was sent to various motive power depots for use as an aid to the adhesion of locomotives on greasy rails or steep gradients. One imagines a fair amount of the stuff must have been used on the Settle & Carlisle itself. Along with Langwathby and Armathwaite, LAZONBY & KIRKOSWALD station re-opened as an unstaffed halt in 1986 following a grant being made by the local authority. An identical twin to that at Langwathby, Lazonby's station building is used as offices by Bells Bakery who also occupy the old goods shed. Once Lazonby's goods yard did a roaring trade in livestock because of the close proximity of an auction mart. In the years following the First World War something like 2,500 cattle wagons were being dealt with per annum. The stationmaster here had forty wage packets to issue every Friday: porters, signalmen, platelayers and the

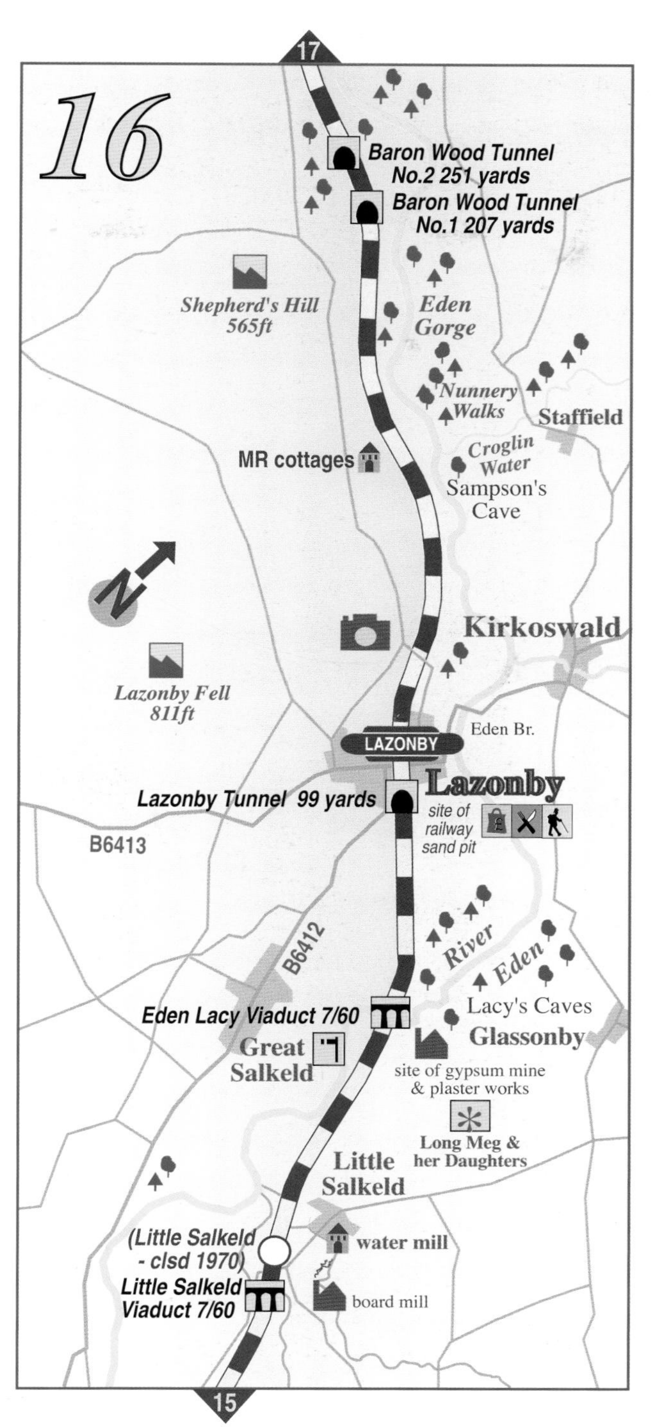

men who worked at the quarry sidings at Long Meg. It is this sense of community and activity that is absent now. Station sauntering, one misses the company of a loquacious porter, the soliloquy of the station stove, the fluttering of pigeons in baskets, the hollow rattle of empty milk churns.

In the heyday of the Midland Railway there was a nightly departure from London St Pancras on the stroke of midnight, a 'Scotch Corridor Express' conveying sleeping car passengers for Glasgow St Enoch. The train reversed at Leeds, acquired a fresh pair of engines, and made its way over the Settle & Carlisle as dawn broke over the Pennine massif. Perhaps many an early riser, inquisitively drawing their compartment blinds as the train snaked its way down the Eden Valley, was fooled into thinking they had already crossed the border, for the scenery hereabouts evokes an uncanny sense of Scotland, especially to the north of Lazonby, as the line winds through the pinewoods of the Eden Gorge. In the vicinity of Baron Wood the line tunnels beneath a brackeny expanse of moorland grazed, as if to heighten the illusion, by herds of Highland cattle. This is hunting, shooting, fishing country personified. On the 'Glorious Twelfth' of 1911 the Midland ran no less than fifteen special trains of sportsmen intent on bagging more than their fair share of grouse.

Another set of isolated sidings can still be seen at BARON WOOD. Here forestry was the raison d'etre, a sawmill cut the timber into pit props which were taken out by rail to various collieries up and down the country. No pit props now and precious few collieries either, one of the present day Settle & Carlisle line's busiest freight traffic flows being imported and opencast coal brought down from Ayrshire in Scotland by train to the power stations of East Yorkshire and the midlands.

The scene from the carriage window between Lazonby and Armathwaite really is ravishing, amply compensating for the loss of mountain scenery. Seen in glimpses between the tunnels and cuttings, the Eden cascades down its rocky bed framed by tumbling woodlands of birch and pine. On the east bank of the river at the point where it is joined by Croglin Water, are the famous Nunnery Walks, a series of pathways stretching down through divine woodlands past a dramatic waterfall and gorge. Hidden from view on the railway line's side of the Eden, close to the Midland cottages at Baron Wood, is Sampson's Chamber, a cave used as a hiding place by a navvy who had murdered one of his colleagues during the building of the railway. Eventually he was captured and hanged at Carlisle.

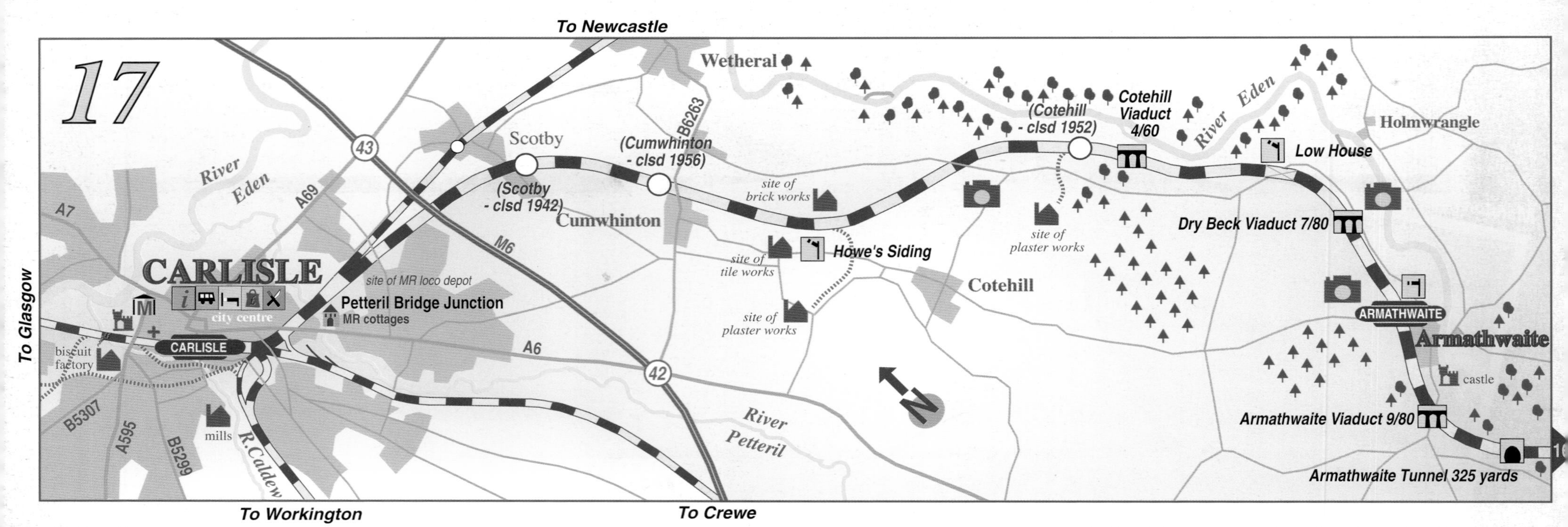

EMERGING from the brief darkness of Armathwaite Tunnel, the line continues to descend before levelling out to cross a curving viaduct, then climbs again to reach ARMATHWAITE station, located in one of the most picturesque settings on the whole of the Settle & Carlisle. Rooks nest noisily in the pines which form a backdrop to the preserved signal box, restored to Midland colours by FoSCL. Far below, the chimney pots and rooftops of the village are glimpsed in a riparian setting. The dominant building is Armathwaite Castle, which had its origins as a pele tower designed to ward off Scots marauders. The station is used now by the British Legion as a club house. Beyond the station precincts, beside the by-road which climbs over the forested shoulder of Hill Rigg, the old stationmaster's house stands in an elevated position alongside some staff cottages.

Noticeably higher above the Eden now, than back at Lazonby and Langwathby, the line progresses northwards over two more lofty viaducts, encountering in the process, a rare level crossing at LOW HOUSE, and passing the three hundred mile marker from London. Three further closed down stations are met on the last lap into Carlisle. A short branch line led from COTEHILL to a plaster works at Knothill. South of Cumwhinton there were sidings serving a variety of industries, notably a brick and tile works, and a plaster and gypsum works; the latter still being shunted by steam in the early Seventies. HOWE'S SIDING signal box is still in use, governing activities on the main line. Once there were thirty-five signal boxes between Settle & Carlisle - currently only six are in regular use.

CUMWHINTON station, closed in 1956, remains in a good state of repair. On 29th December, 1904, a gang of platelayers came upon the carcass of a 'full grown grey male wolf' decapitated by a passing train. Despite local rumours to the contrary, this was not evidence of the survival of such creatures in the wild, but the unsavoury fate of an animal which had escaped from a private zoo. The Midland Railway's most northerly station was SCOTBY, but it closed as early as 1942, the village also being served by a station on the Carlisle-Newcastle line.

As the Settle & Carlisle approaches the border city the Eden, so influential in the line's course and character since Ais Gill, twists away on its roundabout course to the Solway Firth. By rail it's six miles from Cotehill to Carlisle, by river, fourteen! The extremity of the Midland Railway was at PETTERIL BRIDGE JUNCTION, but its trains were granted 'running powers' over the North Eastern tracks into Carlisle station. Interestingly, Bradshaw quoted the distances from Euston and St Pancras to Carlisle respectively as 299 and 308 miles. Without a map, one would have thought that the Midland's wanderings round the East Midlands and the West Riding would have resulted in a significantly larger margin. The London & North Western route via Crewe, however, was much easier and in Edwardian times the LNWR could offer a schedule half an hour faster between London and Carlisle, but the Midland wooed its travelling public with superior rolling stock and delectable scenery.

Your train clatters over pointwork and under the electric catenary of the West Coast main line before coming to rest in the imposing atmosphere of CARLISLE'S 'Citadel' station. High stone walls, the colour of the succulent flesh of Solway sea trout support soaring, pigeon-haunted girders fenestrated by myriad panes of glass. It is a steam age cathedral colonised by the thrumming traction of an era of high technology. A surprising surfeit of railway staff perform mysterious rites and rituals. Rattling trains of parcel trolleys weave intricate patterns between knots of waiting passengers. On platform ends trainspotters gaze at passive rows of locomotives. In Gothic corners travel book writers scribble purple prose on the backs of pocket timetables...

LEEDS HARROGATE YORK

Marston Moor

Knaresborough

Bob Green

Cattal

David Allison

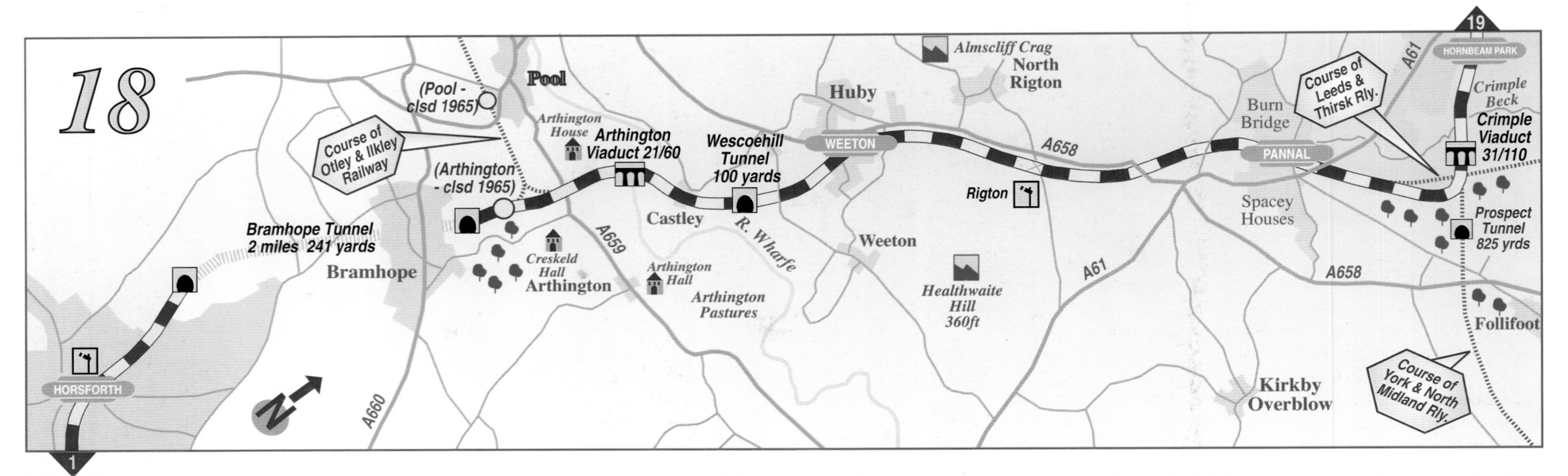

HARROGATE bound trains leave the line to Shipley at Wortley Junction (Map 1) and make their way across the broad valley of the Aire on the 22 curving arches of the Kirkstall Road (or Burley) Viaduct built by the Leeds & Thirsk Railway in 1849. On the far hillside stacked rows of redbrick housing ascend the valley side, characteristic of this quarter of Leeds with their four-storey design with basements and prominent dormer windows, and reminiscent of that fabulous BBC drama series with James Bolam and Barbara Flynn, *The Beiderbecke Affair*. BURLEY PARK station was opened as recently as 1988 and appears to attract much custom from the inhabitants of the neighbourhood.

Engines straining, trains are faced with a steep climb to the summit beyond Horsforth; for the most part the gradient is 1 in 100. Preceded by a short tunnel and ensconced in a land of allotments, HEADINGLEY station has staggered platforms and views over sportsfields to blocks of high rise flats. The famous cricket ground lies to the east of the railway out of sight. Continuing over a high embankment there is a glimpse from the right hand side of the train of a pub going by the curious name of 'Hark to Rover'.

Climbing through woods of silver birch, the line reaches HORSFORTH (Map 18) a staffed station recently provided with attractive new buildings which make good use of traditional materials: stone and slate and glass. In contrast the 19th century North Eastern Railway signal box reminds you that your train will be mechanically signalled all the way to the outskirts of York, and that, indeed, the traditional signalling elements of the journey are one of the most appealing features of travel on this line.

Breasting the summit, almost 500 feet above sea level and amidst rough pastures occupied by grazing horses, the train seems to whoop for joy and plunges into Bramhope Tunnel, over two miles long and the eighth longest in Britain. It took four years to build and accounted for the deaths of twenty-four members of the workforce. These 'unfortunate men' are poignantly remembered by a memorial in Otley churchyard which includes a replica of the impressively decorated northern portal. Making your noisy, subterranean passage through the bore, you can only conjecture as to the nature of the moorland landscape almost 300 feet above, but you will be amused to learn that it features the rugby ground of a club known as the Old Modernarians!

The scene-changers have been busy while you have been left temporarily in the dark. The suburban outskirts of Leeds have been left astern and you have passed into the lovely countryside of Lower Wharfedale. ARTHINGTON station closed in 1965 with the abandonment of the route via Otley to Ilkley, the former stationmaster's house providing a lonely memorial in what was once a triangle of tracks. For many years a 'businessmen's special' ran between Harrogate and Bradford using the north-west chord.

Further confirmation of the Leeds & Thirsk's status as a main line comes with a third substantial engineering structure following the viaduct at Burley and the tunnel at Bramhope; the builders of a branchline could have saved outlay by using the contours and adopting a less direct course. Arthington Viaduct spans the meandering Wharf itself, replicating Burley in its curved nature and considerable count of arches. It is difficult to decide which way to look, for to the west lies The Chevin above Otley, whilst to the east you may catch a glimpse of parkland surrounding Harewood House. Ideally you want to detrain and explore this charming landscape, and you can do just that at the wayside station of WEETON, soon reached through Wescoehill's short tunnel. As the train draws to a halt Almscliff Crag comes into focus a mile to the north-west. This gritstone outcrop may look innocuous, if undoubtably picturesque, but it has been a favoured haunt of rock climbers since the Victorian era.

Rigton's isolated NER signalbox intervenes before

PANNAL is reached, overlooked on one side by a latex foam making factory and on the other by the former station building now converted into a pub. Judging by the number of vehicles occupying the station car park, this is a popular railhead.

Up ahead a substantial viaduct begins to fill the horizon. It would appear to belong to another line crossing yours. There is some truth in this, for Crimple Viaduct was erected by the York & North Midland Railway, part of George Hudson's empire which forged north-westwards, from Church Fenton by way of Wetherby in competition with the Leeds & Thirsk in 1848. The latter originally continued along the valley floor to Starbeck, but a sharply curved chord was built to link the two routes in 1862, by which time both companies had become incorporated in the North Eastern Railway.

Wheels squealing in protest at the tightness of curve, the train ascends through swarthy cuttings of bracken and birch to join the sadly long defunct line from Wetherby, then moves out on to Crimple Viaduct, all thirty-one arches of it. Soon

The graceful curves of Arthington Viaduct carry the Leeds to Harrogate line across the River Wharfe.

you are crossing over the trackbed of the Leeds & Thirsk route, abandoned as a through line in 1951, and then there are panoramic views across the Great Yorkshire Showground towards the conspicuous spire of a church at Knaresborough, beyond which, on clear days, the Hambleton Hills and the Kilburn White Horse can be discerned, all of twenty-five miles away. HORNBEAM PARK, with staggered platforms, was opened to serve a business park and college in 1992. As you pull away, look out for an overgrown cutting on the left-hand side which once led to Brunswick station, Harrogate's original railway terminus opened by the York & North Midland Railway in 1848, but abandoned when the more centrally located station in use today was brought into use fourteen years later. You may just also discern the portal of a former tunnel adapted for use during the Second World War as an air-raid shelter.

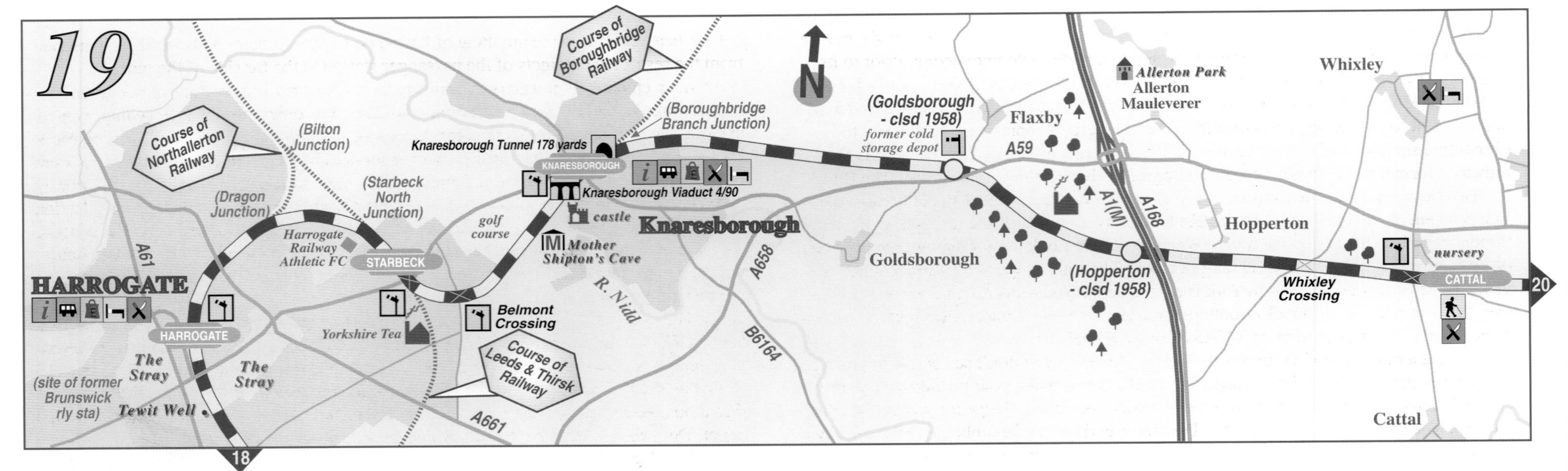

AFFORDING tantalising glimpses of The Stray - two hundred acres of delightful green-belt within the town boundary - the train slows for HARROGATE. A small domed cupola is glimpsed: it covers Tewit Well, the first source of Harrogate water to be exploited for its medicinal properties, as early as the 16th century.

In the golden age of railways the "Harrogate Sunday Pullman's" pampered passengers would be anticipating the challenge of securing the services of a porter. Today our preoccupations are more mundane and the station's present architecture echoes this fall from grace, reflecting poorly on the spa town on its doorstep. Rationalisation has reduced the number of trains and platforms, whilst ungainly office-blocks and multi-storey car parks create an inappropriate impression. If only Harrogate had been blessed with one of the North Eastern Railway's trademark grandiose train sheds along the lines of Hull, York, Darlington and Newcastle, it might yet have a station to be proud of.

Neither has Harrogate been fortuitous with regard to the evolution of its rail services. A half-hourly commuter link with Leeds and Knaresborough, an hourly connection with York, and a weekday express to and from London might appear adequate until you realise that, were it not for some key closures in the 1960s, Harrogate could well be plugged into the Trans-Pennine express network. Time and time again it becomes apparent wherever you travel by train in the UK, that Beeching's greater sin was not so much the withdrawal of services, as the rapid and irreversible obliteration of the routes they used. The strict financial argument for closure of the Wetherby line in 1964 and the Northallerton line three years later may have been irrefutable, but if the trackbeds of those routes had been retained intact, and the railways subsequently reinstated towards the end of the 20th century, as population growth and road traffic congestion impacted, transport in the region would be in a far more cohesive state now. Incidentally, there were once local passenger services from bay platforms at the north end of Harrogate station to Pateley Bridge in the Nidd Valley and Boroughbridge and Pilmoor (on the East Coast Main Line south of Thirsk) until the early 1950s, being the victims of competition from the area's burgeoning post-war bus network.

Mulling over such matters of myopic transport planning, you pull out of Harrogate station under the watchful eye of an early post-war signal box and an imposing, though much pruned, gantry of semaphore signals. Typically an ASDA supermarket occupies the site of Harrogate's former goods yard, there being no hint of rail freight in the district for many years. Stone-built terraced housing borders one side of the line - belying the spa's more graciously perceived architectural style - before the train curves disconcertingly southwards in the direction of Starbeck. At Dragon Junction, the course of the line to Ripon and Northallerton still keeps the housing at bay, finding use as a cycle path now. This was no by-way, the "Queen of Scots" used this line on the long journey between Glasgow Queen Street and London Kings Cross. Picture it, leaning into the curve, a Peppercorn 'Pacific' at the front end, the epitome of Pullman travel in the final years of steam. At the end of 2003 a £40,000 feasibility study was being undertaken to establish what impact reinstatement of the Harrogate-Northallerton railway might have on transport, the environment and the economy of this part of North Yorkshire, and there is a good degree of support within local authorities for the railway to be re-established.

Daunted by the need for a steep climb to the town, the Leeds & Thirsk Railway ignored Harrogate, providing a station instead at STARBECK, opened in 1848. The site of Starbeck North Junction marks the original course of the line northwards. Starbeck became a railway centre of some standing, archive photographs depict a station with lengthy platforms protected by voluminous canopies, and here were marshalling yards and a motive power depot whose drivers and firemen owned to a wide route knowledge. Prior to its closure in 1959, Starbeck, coded 50D, had significant allocations of Gresley's 4-4-0 D49 and 0-6-0 D39 classes. In its heyday the railway must have been an important source of employment. Now the station is unstaffed and the deep canopies have given way to diminutive shelters. Only in the name of the adjoining non-league football club is the railway's former status remembered - Harrogate Railway Athletic: "come on 'The Rail'!"

Two busy road crossings ensure survival of a pair of mechanical signal boxes - the first substantial, the other tiny - as the line to York twists towards the north-east and heads through wooded cuttings on the way to Knaresborough. Look out for the modern premises of Yorkshire Tea with its amusing tea-pot clock! The train drops at 1 in 105 towards the Nidd Gorge and milepost 17 from York is passed before you suddenly find yourself soaring over the river and steeply huddled rooftops, on a level with the church tower and the castle's ruined keep, into the confines of KNARESBOROUGH station.

You get a bird's eye view from the viaduct. But what you don't see is this imposing structure in the grandeur of its setting. Cue to alight and make your way down quaintly cobbled Water Bag Bank to the river to be in a better position to judge for yourself whether the famous architectural critic Nikolaus Pevsner was right to take umbrage at the railway's impact on the scene. In his opinion it is 'one of the most notable railway crimes in England', and he added, somewhat crushingly, that 'to castellate a bridge does not make it a picturesque object'! Doubtless he would have been happier if, following its collapse before completion in 1848, it hadn't been re-erected. By most tenets of good taste, however, Knaresborough Viaduct is one of Britain's most beautiful railway bridges, an holistic response from its Victorian builders to the majesty of its location.

Squeezed into the tightest of spaces between the viaduct and a tunnel, Knaresborough's railway station could easily have been an afterthought. In truth it's aesthetically very satisfying, charming in its use of yellow brick, its low roofs embellished by high chimneys and wooden ventilators. The canopies are very pretty too and enhanced by hanging baskets - a long timber bench provides plenty of room for weary bottoms on the down platform. The station is unmanned, but you wouldn't think it, because a bistro and a shop specialising in antique and replica fireplaces create a sense of humanity. In fact, the sole railwayman in Knaresborough now is the signalman who descends from his quaint eyrie (reminiscent of a similar arrangement at Snettisham in Norfolk in being flush with the end of a stone terrace of houses) to present the driver of York-bound trains with a token for the single-line section to Cattal.

Until the autumn of 1950, rail travellers journeying east of Knaresborough had a choice of routes. The alternative to the obvious choice of York was a branchline which wended its way across the Ure at Boroughbridge and the Swale at Brafferton to reach the East Coast Main Line at Pilmoor. A railway backwater if ever there was one, and yet had its promoters ambitions been realised it might have developed into a trunk route between the West Riding and the Yorkshire Coast. Hardly any sign remains of the Boroughbridge line, which remained open for goods as far as Boroughbridge until 1964. Similarly, you have to look hard and fast to see anything of Knaresborough's former goods facilities, banished from the restricted precincts of the passenger station to the far side of the tunnel.

A steep embankment ushers the railway over the retreating rooftops of suburban Knaresborough and out into an emptying landscape of quiet farmland. Beeching wanted to close this line. Several of its remoter stations - Goldsborough, Hopperton, Marston Moor and Hessay - had already lost their passenger services in 1958, but enough objections were received for closure to be deferred. Singling of the track took place in the 1970s, a curiously ill-conceived attempt to modernise when one considers that it necessitated the introduction of token working, and thus the retention of signalmen. Furthermore, as it crosses the pancake flat Vale of York, the railway encounters many level crossings, all of which retain hand-operated gates and therefore require the costly - though charmingly quaint - employment of crossing-keepers.

At GOLDSBOROUGH the Ministry of Food erected a cold storage depot during the Second World War. After the war it saw use as a bacon factory. It's still extant, in industrial use, though no longer rail-linked naturally. Trains tend to get up to quite a useful speed along this stretch, but you might just glimpse the former station buildings and the 'austerity' signal box, no longer in railway use, which dates from the installation of the cold storage depot. Donnelley's large factory alongside the line produces directories in their millions for Yellow Pages. There was talk when the plant opened of providing a siding for delivering vast quantities of paper by rail, but then that's what we tend to do best in this country - talk.

Before the A1 bridge was built, long queues of traffic inevitably occurred when the signalman at HOPPERTON closed the gates to effect the passage of trains. Cream-washed now, the station building remains, in residential use. Flocks of sheep and domestic geese, copses and coverts, characterise the countryside as the line reaches CATTAL and becomes double track again. A hand-operated level crossing hinders traffic on a north-south by-road which follows the course of a Roman Road. Skirted by nursery gardens, Cattal exemplifies the architectural style of the East & West Yorkshire Railway, or at least the stations at Hopperton, Cattal, Marston Moor and Poppleton which were considered the most important when the line was being built. In each case, the main building provided accommodation for the station master as well as space for a waiting room, booking hall and offices. Brick was the main material adopted, but stone quoins lend additional dignity. Under the eaves space was provided for a station clock, but apparently none were ever inserted, for they were running over budget - time was obviously money!

At Cattal the quaint timber signal box is a North Eastern Railway replacement for a ground-frame of a design still in place at Hammerton. These days, of course, the station building is in private hands, but it's heartening to come upon a comfortable waiting-room, hermetically sealed from Nidd Valley breezes and boasting comfortable seats and a choice of reading matter which would put some doctor's surgeries to shame. A timber goods shed remains intact on the up platform, whilst the down is enhanced by a picturesque clump of Scots pine. Yes, considering that this is the 21st century, Cattal continues to exude much of the charm of the wayside station of folklore.

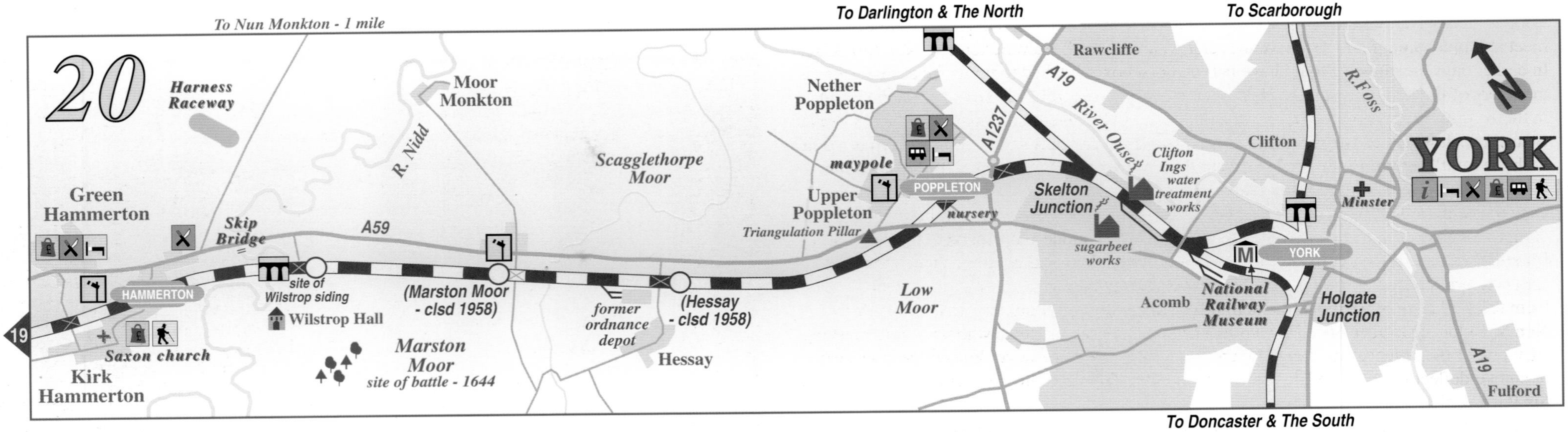

FLAT - and thereby the antithesis of Settle & Carlisle country - the fertile landscape of the lower Nidd valley merges with the alluvial Vale of York, a low-horizoned infinity of fields. Ella Pontefract and Marie Hartley, those indefatigable explorers and chroniclers of Yorkshire between the two world wars, called it in *Yorkshire Tour* a 'sunken, quiet land, out of the beaten track, with hedges bordering green fields, trees overhanging winding roads, and here and there a circle of willows round a still green pond'.

Flat, yes, but *not* dull; and waiting for a train on HAMMERTON'S charmingly remote (but healthily frequented) wayside station can be a soothing experience. Between its deep banks, the river winds its way past Wilstrop Wood, beyond which lies Marston Moor, scene on July 2nd, 1644 of one of the Civil War's most definitive battles. Prince Rupert, King Charles's nephew had marched the Cavaliers from Shrewsbury to confront Cromwell's Roundhead army in the neighbourhood of York, a city under siege. Early in the battle Cromwell was wounded but, having had his wound dressed, rejoined his men and decisively fell upon a wing of the Royalist cavalry in the vicinity of Wilstrop Wood. By the end of the day some four thousand Royalists were dead. By comparison the three hundred Parliamentarians lost seemed a small price to pay, though they failed to capitalize on their victory and the Civil War dragged on for another couple of years.

Three centuries later warfare of an altogether different nature brought the activity of a military aerodrome to the neighbourhood. One imagines many an airman alighted at Hammerton or Cattal to commence a tour of duty at RAF Marston Moor, a training station for Bomber Command from 1941 onwards. Leonard Cheshire was Station Commander at the base in 1943 when his seminal book *Bomber Pilot* first appeared in print.

The line singles east of Hammerton and spans the Nidd on a low-slung viaduct of iron construction. The river is just a couple of miles short of its confluence with the Ouse at Nun Monkton. Within sight of the railway, the A59 York to Skipton road crosses the river as well, the classical early 19th century cut-watered arches of Skip Bridge having been by-passed by a regretably blander modern structure.

Wilstrop existed primarily for agricultural produce, its single siding, trailing in the York direction, serving a curiously open covered shed not unlike a Dutch barn. According to the July 1922 *Bradshaw* the 11am from Harrogate would deign to call on Saturdays to take prospective passengers to York and return them and their bulging shopping-bags on the 3.22pm from the minster city. The station house remains intact and the crossing is still in use providing access to Wilstrop Hall, the sole railwayman ensconced in a portacabin for his pains.

Marston Moor and Hessay lost their passenger services in 1958, but at both locations the station buildings remain in residential use, the former offering bed & breakfast facilities. At both sites there are manually operated level-crossings. At Hessay a former Ministry of Defence depot has been redeveloped for industrial use, rendering its former sidings obsolete.

The majority of passenger services between Harrogate and York were dieselised with multiple units in 1959, Birmingham R.C. & W. (latterly 104) and Metro-Cammell (101) types predominating. Their introduction might have appealed to the travelling public, railway staff and management respectively, but it did largely bring to an end the use of Sir Nigel Gresley's handsome D49 class 4-4-0's on the route. They were named after fox-hunts in LNER territory; a contentious matter now of course, but resonant in those days of the rural locales they worked in. Their brass nameplates sported a cast figure of a fox above the lettering, and it would be nice to think that Reynard approved of this feature, and indeed railways generally, it being a part of country lore that many a fox cunningly used the scent of creosoted sleepers to throw a pack of hounds off his scent.

The Harrogate to York line ran across the territory of the

York & Ainsty Hunt; more particularly that of its 'North' pack of hounds, who still regularly meet at Goldsborough, Allerton Mauleverer, Whixley, Kirk Hammerton and Nun Monkton. In earlier days the railway would have laid on horseboxes hitched to trains for more far-flung members of the hunt to reach the meet. But according to a full page advertisement placed in the *York & Ainsty Hunt Annual* by the 1930s the LNER were offering 'Road Motor Horse Boxes' which would convey horses from their stables to the meet and thereafter 'keep in touch with the hunt', returning the tired steeds to their homes at the conclusion of the day's run. Further details were obtainable by telephoning York 2671, and no doubt the line was kept busy throughout the hunting calendar; whilst, admirable as many of the train operating companies are today, one can't quite see them laying on modern horseboxes for the hunting fraternity as part of their franchise renewal bids. Two additional equine connections in the area concern the existence of York's Harness Raceway on the no through road which runs from the A59 at Hammerton to the delightful village of Nun Monkton; and the naming of Nun Monkton's pub after *Alice Hawthorn*, a famous 19th century mare who won an astonishing fifty-one of the seventy-one races she entered. Sadly her name never graced the splashers or smoke-deflectors of an LNER Pacific, though her direct breeding line produced *Ladas* and *Sir Visto*, which did.

Running across a shallow embankment over Low Moor, and accompanied by telegraph poles alas no longer strung with wire, the line heads for POPPLETON. In the June 1955 issue of *Trains Illustrated*, the celebrated Poppleton-based train-timer P. W. B. Semmens described a footplate ride on an ancient North Eastern Railway D20 4-4-0 one wet and windy night with the 5.30 p.m. York to Harrogate 'express': 'the boiler was steaming beautifully and the pressure rose from 175 lb. at Poppleton to 185 lb. when the safety valves lifted'.

Entering a shallow cutting, before passing beneath the A59, the line passes a triangulation pillar unusually located within the railway boundary. Either side of the line there is more evidence of nursery gardening. These are the glass-houses of Poppleton Nursery, where many a railway station hanging basket has been nurtured over the years, materials being moved about the premises by narrow gauge railway. Sadly, less use is being made of it now, as is apparent by the empty character of many of the glass-houses, though the nursery does reputedly still provide flowers and plants for a number of Settle & Carlisle stations.

Poppleton's level crossing retains its cabin and traditional wooden gates, and features a two-platformed station whose architectural styling you will recognise as being typical of the East & West Yorkshire Railway. The signalman dexterously collects the token as the line re-doubles. As befits a suburban railhead for York, trade here is brisk, and you sense that Poppleton folk find the train an enjoyable and stress-free method of reaching the frequently grid-locked city centre. As the train pulls out on the last leg of its journey, keep your eyes peeled for the charming flower bed on the down platform with the station's name spelt out in whitewashed lettering made from stone.

Skelton Junction is marked for miles ahead by the steam fluming from a sugar beet factory's tall chimney which has long acted as a weather-vane for York's amateur meteorologists. On to the historic tracks of the East Coast Main Line your diesel unit humbly trundles, in the august wheelprints of Edward Fletcher, Vincent Raven, Nigel Gresley, Edward Thompson, Arthur Peppercorn and the self-effacing team at Vulcan Factory who designed the peerless Deltics. As the slow lines, used by freight trains, twist away to avoid York station, the train runs in past engineering yards and comes alongside the River Ouse. The Minster comes into view and, on the far bank of the river, St Peter's School, founded in 627 (as every trainspotter above the age of fifty will remember) by dint of it having the Gresley V2 Class 60847 named after it. Its alumni range from Guy Fawkes to the humble author of this guide: though, despite appearances to the contrary, and the toll that the ageing process has inevitably taken, the two men were not (regardless of the visual evidence suggested by the photograph reproduced above) in the same year.

Puccino's, York

Karen Tanguy

On the right hand side of the train stands the National Railway Museum, occupying the site (and, indeed, some of the buildings) of York's main locomotive depot, 50A. The Scarborough line comes in from the left upon a handsome bridge spanning the Ouse, as York's famous curving train shed reaches enthusiastically out to embrace you, in a ferrous hug of welcome. Its vast bulk shelters sharply curving platforms, and the Harrogate train shudders to a halt at the one numbered '8'. 'This is York'. 'This is York': not so much 'all change' as *plus ca change ...*

If there is a moral and theme to the *Iron Roads* series, it is that you should go by rail wherever possible, but that once aboard your train, you should not sit slavishly on it, but that should get off and explore at intervening stations as often as your schedule allows. We are not Egon Ronay, we are not the National Park Authority we are not the local Chamber of Commerce, all the facilities and suggestions listed in this Gazetteer are merely launch pads for your individual devlopment and enthusiasm. To the best of our knowledge the entries are accurate at the time of going to press, but we would urge you to use the telephone or internet to check ahead of your visit for your own peace of mind. Make good use of the local Tourist Information Centres, invariably courteous and models of patience and humour in the face of the most inane enquiry. Have fun!

Appleby *Map 14*

Until 1974 the county borough of Westmorland, Appleby is one of the most interesting and historic small towns in northern England. There is no better way to arrive here (other, perhaps, than by Gypsy vado) than by train along the Settle & Carlisle. The centre of town lies across the gorgeous Eden, a pleasant five minute walk downhill from the station. The main thoroughfare - Boroughgate - sweeps imposingly down from the castle to the market square. Bordered by lawns and lime trees, it exudes an unostentatious dignity. At either end stand obelisks topped by sundials. Known as High Cross and Low Cross respectively, they marked the trading boundaries of the market. At the upper end of Boroughgate an archway leads to a courtyard of almhouses built for the widows of the town by Lady Anne Clifford in 1651 and serving the same sublime function to this day. The main building at the foot of Boroughgate is the 16th century Moot Hall. Beyond it a row of cloisters attractively screen the approach to the parish church of St Lawrence.

Appleby lets its otherwise well-permed, blue-rinsed hair down once a year for the famous Horse Fair on the second Wednesday in June. Gypsies and traders, travelling folk and tourists descend in droves for up to a week beforehand, many of them camping out on Fair Hill to the east of the railway station. Traditional vados, or horse-drawn vans, share the camping ground with luxury trailers. Stalls are set up and fortunes told. Over evening camp fires can be heard the lilt of Romany music. But behind all the bonhomie, the business of buying and selling horses is taken earnestly, and the animals are taken down to the Eden for a wash, an altogether picturesque sight in an altogether picturesque town.

Accommodation

TUFTON ARMS HOTEL - Market Square. Tel: 017683 51593. Comfortably old fashioned, family run 3 star hotel 5 minutes walk from the station. Fishing rights on the River Eden.

GOLDEN BALL - High Wiend. Tel: 017683 51493. CAMRA recommended local just off the main thoroughfare. Food and accommodation. Jennings beers from Cockermouth.

MIDLAND HOTEL - adjacent station. Outwardly dour but inwardly snug little local, ideal for a quick drink or snack between trains. Inexpensive B&B Tel: 017683 51524.

Eating & Drinking

RIVERSIDE FISH & CHIPS - The Sands. Tel: 017683 51464. Excellent fish & chip shop adjacent to the town bridge just 3 minutes from the station.

Things to Do

TOURIST INFORMATION - Moot Hall, Boroughgate. Tel: 017683 51177. *www.visiteden.co.uk*

Shopping

Market day on Fridays, early closing on Thursdays. Farmers Market 1st Saturday in the month. Branches of HSBC and Barclays banks. Some fine food outlets jostle for space with gift shops.

Connections

BUSES - Useful connections with Penrith, Keswick, Brough and Barnard Castle. Tel: 0870 608 2 608. Some services run to and from the railway station. Check when you enquire about times. TAXIS - JVR Taxis. Tel: 017683 52382. AJ Taxis - Tel: 07793 126 222.

Walking

Good walking country, along the Eden Valley, Dufton Pike or Great Dun Fell, trawl the TIC for leaflets and walking guides. Appleby is also often used as a starting point for guided walks from the railway - further details locally or from the TIC.

Armathwaite *Map 17*

On a warm summer's day there is no finer Settle & Carlisle destination than Armathwaite. Eschew the temptation to swelter with the tourist crowds of Carlisle, alight here instead and treat yourself to lunch in one or other of the two comfortable inns, then spend the rest of your time lazing by the river bank watching the fat Eden salmon rising for flies. The suffix 'thwaite' echoes the Norse origins of this peaceful village, for whom salmon netting was once the most significant economic activity. An 18th century sandstone bridge spans the river at the site of an earlier ford. The tiny sandstone church has a stained glass window designed by Burne-Jones. Useful village stores and Post Office offering teas.

Eating, Drinking & Accommodation

DUKES HEAD HOTEL - Front Street. Bar & restaurant meals, teas & coffees; accommodation. Tel: 016974 72226.

FOX & PHEASANT HOTEL - far side of river bridge. Small hotel characterised by oak beams and slate floors. Meals and accommodation. Cumbria-brewed Jennings and Hesket Newmarket ales. Tel: 01694 72400.

Bentham *Map 6*

Unless it's Wednesday, and the cattle market's in full swing, visitors have to make their own entertainment in Bentham, but that's not to denigrate this worthwhile staging post on the Lancaster Line. Alight here and you can make your way southwards to see the Great Stone of Fourstones (there used to be three others but they were snapped up by enterprising local stonemasons as building material) or follow the River Wenning, upstream to Clapham or downstream to Wennington.

Eating & Drinking

THE NOSEBAG - Main Street. Coffee shop with occasional bistro evenings. Tel: 01542 63150.

ASIAN SPICE - Main Street. Balti restaurant and take-away. Tel: 01542 63400.

Also several pubs, a Chinese and an Irish (!) fish & chip shop.

Shopping

Surprisingly good range of facilities including two general stores, three banks, butchers, bakers, gift and outdoor clothing shops and a post office all located within easy reach of the station.

Connections

BUSES - Stagecoach services Mon-Sat to/from the tourist town of Ingleton. Tel: 0870 608 2 608.

Bingley *Map 2*

The recently opened Airedale Relief Road has siphoned a good deal of traffic away from Bingley's town centre, to the obvious relief of its citizens if not its shop-keeper's. One interesting feature is the Butter Cross and Market Hall. King John gave the town its first market charter in 1212. The riverside is surprisingly pleasant in the vicinity of the church.

Eating & Drinking

BROWN COW - Ireland Bridge. Tel: 01274 569482. Timothy Taylors pub attractively located on the far bank of the Aire.

VECCHIO MULINO - Park Road. Tel: 01274 770533. Sardinian restaurant and sandwich bar.

Shopping

Market on Wednesdays and Fridays. Early closing on Tuesdays. DAMART factory shop on Park Road - Tel: 01274 568211.

Walking

Via Cross Gates and the Druid's Altar to Thwaites Brow and Keighley (4 miles), or by way of the canal past 'Five Rise Locks' to Micklethwaite and across the top of Ilkley Moor to Ilkley (6 miles) from where you can catch the train back to Shipley.

Carlisle *Map 17*

Carlisle was always the sort of place you passed through on the way to somewhere else. Generations of railway travellers were left with memories of engines being changed and wheel-tappers at work. Motorists retained a blurred impression of suburban villas strung out along the A6. Nowadays, though, the 'Border City' sets out its stall as a tourist destination in its own right, somewhere well capable of sustaining your interest on a day out, or a strategic base from which to explore the rich variety of landscapes to be found on its doorstep: the Tyne Valley and Hadrian's Wall; the Eden Valley and the Pennines; the Lake District, the Cumbrian Coast and the Scottish Borders. Fortunately most of these areas remain well served by rail, the Waverley route to Hawick and Edinburgh being Carlisle's only major railway loss. Of all these railway connections, Carlisle has benefitted most - financillay and ambiently - from the explosion of tourism associated with the Settle & Carlisle. The circular towers of the Citadel, which face the station exit, set the tone for this architecturally well endowed city. Beyond them the visitor can follow English Street to the pedestrianised Market Square, where the old town hall has been refurbished as an excellent Tourist Information Centre, a good point of departure for closer exploration of this immensely likeable place.

Accommodation

LAKES COURT HOTEL - Court Square. Tel: 012248 531951. Comfortably refurbished Victorian hotel handily placed beside the railway station. Restaurant open to non-residents.

IBIS HOTEL - Botchergate. Tel: 01228 518000. Modern 'travel-lodge' style accommodation a few hundred yards from the station.

CROWN & MITRE - English Street. Three star hotel in city centre yet less than 5 minutes walk from the station. Tel: 01228 525491.

Eating & Drinking

PRIORS KITCHEN - Cathedral Close. Pleasant crypt-located cafe for coffees, light lunches and teas (closed Sundays) Tel: 01228 543251.

PIERRE'S BISTRO - Lowther Street. French restaurant, once part of the Victoire chain. Tel: 01228 515111.

PANCHO'S CAFE BAR - Court Square. Tel: 01228 515379. Mexican/Spanish cafe/restaurant in the square outside the railway station.

LEONARDO'S - Lonsdale Street. Tel: 01228 542014. Mediterranean cuisine.

CUMBERLAND INN - Botchergate. Tel: 01228 536900. Characterful drinking-hole close to the station (turn right out of square) retaining echoes of Carlisle's unique State Management scheme and also featuring railwayana.

Things to Do

CARLISLE VISITOR CENTRE - Old Town Hall. Tel: 01228 625600.

TULLIE HOUSE - Castle Street. Much vaunted celebration of Carlisle and The Borders turbulent history, including section devoted to the city's railway heyday. Open daily. Tel: 01228 534781.

CASTLE - Castle Way. Well preserved fortification dating from 11th century. Tel: 01228 591922.

CATHEDRAL - Castle Street. Tel: 01228 548151. 12th century church built from an attractive shade of red sandstone. One of the country's lesser known ecclesiastical treasures.

Shopping

Carlisle is an excellent regional centre, and in THE LANES (Tel: 01228 529356) shopping centre they have managed to create a modern precinct of considerable character. To our way of thinking, however, pride of place should go to the delightful COVERED MARKET, a Victorian retailing centre rivalling Citadel station in its architectural splendour. It houses a fine array of stalls, many specialising in Cumbrian delicacies. In Castle Street, BOOKCASE is one of the best second-hand bookshops and classical CD centres in the provinces - Tel: 01228 544560.

Connections

BUSES - Tel: 0870 608 2 608.

TAXIS - Tel: 01228 520000, 527575, 523971.

CAR HIRE - Hertz have an office on the station. Tel: 01228 524273.

Dent

Carnforth *Map 7*

The station's regeneration has had a beneficial knock-on effect on the town which seems much livelier than in the recent past. But it's mostly for its role as a transport centre that Carnforth continues to be known, and you've the opportunity here to explore the scenic Lancaster Canal or change trains for the highly enjoyable Furness Line route to Barrow and beyond.

Accommodation, Eating & Drinking

ROYAL STATION HOTEL - Market Street. Tel: 01524 732033. Two star hotel across the road from the railway station.

BRIEF ENCOUNTER REFRESHMENT ROOM - Railway Station. Baguettes, omelettes and salads with a liberal helping of instant nostalgia. Tel: 01524 732432.

Shopping

A growing range of shops reflects Carnforth's growing relationship with tourism. In the station itself you'll come upon STATION CURIOS & CARDS (Tel: 01524 823587), STATION MODELS (Tel: 01524 730404), BAY MODELS (which specialise in garden railways - Tel: 01524 730101), and HERITANCE (for heraldry, horoscopes and tapestry - Tel: 01524 720333). Further up Market Street, the main thoroughfare, is MADDISON'S, a butcher and prize-winning sausage maker (Tel: 01524 732021) and the excellent CARNFORTH BOOKSHOP (Tel: 01524 734588) which stocks new books as well as a large collection of antiquarian stock.

Connections

BUSES - services along the Lune Valley to Kirkby Lonsdale and along the coast to Morecambe. Further details from the Carnforth Connect office on the railway station - Tel: 01524 734311.

Cattal *Map 19*

Halfway between Cattal to the south and the larger settlement of Whixley to the north, the railway station is more a useful commuter railhead than a jumping-off point for tourists.

Clapham *Map 6*

Gorgeous village nestling under the flank of Ingleborough, but the best part of half an hour's walk away from its lonely station.

Dent *Map 11*

A northern Clovelly, but with the character of mint cake rather than the cloying nature of cream fudge, Dent huddles under the shoulders of the fells, its houses cuddled together to protect themselves from the elements. Cobbled streets wind past ancient, whitewashed buildings and somehow, despite its popularity with tourists, the village retains a sense of reality, of a community going about its daily business. Business now is farming and tourism, but a couple of centuries ago Dent was a centre for the making of gloves and stockings. The inhabitants were then known as the 'terrible knitters of Dent': not a reflection on their aptitude, but terrible in the sense of a great capacity for work. The trade relied on packhorse trains for the carriage into the village of wool and worsted and the export out of finished goods. but the development of a mechanised woollen industry in the West Riding, better connected by canal and then railway to the rest of the country, doomed Dent to a spiral of decline.

Eating, Drinking & Accommodation

GEORGE & DRAGON HOTEL - Main Street. Tel: 015396 25256. Comfortable country inn offering accommodation and bar or restaurant meals washed down with their own Dent Brewery beer.

SUN INN - Main Street. Classic country pub, comfortably furnished and blissfully free from piped music (even the juke-box is consigned discreetly to the games room) relying on the best pub ambience of all - the hubbub of people's voices. Home-cooked bar meals and locally-brewed Dent Brewery ales. Tel: 015396 25208.

STONE CLOSE CAFE - Main Street. Mike Harding has called this 'the best little cafe in the Dales' and we share his enthusiasm. Wide range of fresh,

continued overleaf

continued from page 47
mouthwatering food. Warm fires for winter's walkers. Accommodation also available. Tel: 015396 25231.
SPORTSMANS INN - Cowgill Tel: 015396 25282. Dent Brewery beers, food and accommodation. Family-owned county inn idyllically located beside the River Dee a mile from the station. Nicknamed 'The Dub'.
YOUTH HOSTEL - Cowgill. Tel: 015396 25251. Former shooting lodge which has been a hostel since 1944. Two miles walk (downhill) from the station.

Shopping
Post office and general store; gallery, wool shop and craft shop.

Connections
TAXIS - Tel: 015396 25297.

Walking
Dent can be reached on foot from the station via Cowgill and the "Dales Way" (5 miles) or, more adventurously, from Ribblehead and across the back of Whernside (7 miles).

Gargrave *Map 4*

The River Aire waters the village green, flowing seductively beneath a three-arch bridge past stone cottages built at apparent random to the main street. Gargrave straddles the "Pennine Way" and a proliferation of shops and cafes cater for this passing trade.

Eating & Drinking
DALESMAN CAFE - village centre. Tel: 01756 749250. High starch meals for hungry cyclists and walkers.
BOLLYWOOD COTTAGE - village centre. Tel: 01756 749252. Indian restaurant and take-away.

Walking
Good centre for walking sections of the Pennine Way and Leeds & Liverpool Canal.

Garsdale *Map 11*

A scattered community with no real centre. The railway station is actually located at Garsdale Head where there are lines of former railway staff cottages, a number of isolated farms, a Mount Zion chapel and an inn.

Accommodation, Eating & Drinking
THE MOORCOCK INN - approximately a mile from the station at the junction of the Sedbergh-Hawes and Kirkby Stephen roads. Bar meals and bed & breakfast. Tel: 01969 667488.

Connections
Tuesdays only bus link with Hawes - Tel: 0870 608 2 608.

Walking
To Grisedale and Uldale - both off the beaten track - or to Hawes via Tarn Hill, Cotterdale and the Pennine Way.

Giggleswick *Map 6*

Scattered quarrying village separated from Settle by the River Ribble. Famous for its public school (dating from 1512) whose copper domed chapel is a local landmark. Giggleswick Scar marks the Craven Fault Line. Edward Elgar, an occasional guest of a local practitioner, Charles William Buck, walked along the scar and played golf on the local course here in the 1880s. Settle town centre (and all its facilities) is only a mile from Giggleswick station, near which is a road-side plague stone used to disinfect money in Tudor times. The Ribble Way passes through Giggleswick on its 70 mile course from Longton, near Preston to Gavel Gap near Ribblehead.

Accommodation and Eating & Drinking
THE BLACK HORSE - village centre. 17th century inn adjoining pretty church. Food and accommodation. Tel: 01729 822506.

Shopping
Post office stores plus good secondhand bookshop called POST HORN BOOKS - Tel: 01729 823438.

Hammerton *Map 20*

The station serves the two distinct villages of Kirk Hammerton and Green Hammerton, the former with its notable Saxon church being closer to the railway. Frustratingly, there's a dearth of public footpaths, particularly in the vicinity of the Nidd. Those equipped with bicycles can, however, find their way to the picturesque village of Nun Monkton a couple of country miles north-east of Hammerton station. On arrival, they'll discover a delightful village grouped lazily about a broad green with archetypal duck pond and maypole. The church, once part of a nunnery, has glass by Burne-Jones.

Accommodation, Eating & Drinking
BAY HORSE INN - Green Hammerton. Tel: 01423 330338. Comfortable country pub offering accommodation, bar and restaurant meals.
GRAVELEYS - A59 adjacent to Skip Bridge. Branch of famous Harrogate fish & chip restaurant; take-aways also. Tel: 01423 330992.

Kirk Hammerton

ALICE HAWTHORN - Nun Monkton. Unspoilt country pub. Home-made food, Timothy Taylors and Camerons beer. Tel: 01423 330303.

Shopping
Post office stores in the centres of both villages plus well-stocked SPAR at garage on A59.

Harrogate *Map 19*

Seminars and conferences have supplanted taking the waters as Harrogate's stock in trade, but this is still a hugely elegant spa town blessed by its wide open spaces and gardens.

Accommodation
HARROGATE BRASSERIE HOTEL - Cheltenham Parade. Tel: 01423 505041. Two star accommodation, restaurant, live jazz and North Yorkshire brewed Hambleton Ales.
CUTLERS ON THE STRAY - West Park. Tel: 01423 524471. Stylish bar, brasserie and three star accommodation overlooking The Stray.
TRAVEL INN - Hornbeam Park. Tel: 08701 977 126. Travel lodge style accommodation handily placed beside Hornbeam Park station on the southern outskirts of Harrogate.

Eating & Drinking
BETTYS - Parliament Street. Tel: 01423 502746. A Harrogate institution not to be missed, though its very popularity often means you'll need to queue to get a table. Open 9am-9pm daily; piano accompaniment 6pm-9pm. Exquisite marquetry by the Alsatian Spindlers.
PINNOCHIO'S - Cheltenham Parade. Tel: 01423 560611. Lively Italian restaurant housed in lavishly decorated former theatre.
GRAVELEY'S - Cheltenham Parade. Tel: 01423 507093. Traditional fish & chips and seafood restaurant.
SOUS LA TABLE - Cheltenham Parade. Tel: 01423 565806. Classic French cuisine.
COACH & HORSES - West Park. Tel: 01423 568371. Convivial CAMRA recommended pub overlooking The Stray. Lunchtime food and a wide choice of Yorkshire beers.

Things to Do
TOURIST INFORMATION CENTRE - Royal Baths. Tel: 01423 537300.
ROYAL PUMP ROOM - Royal Parade. Tel: 01423 556188. Local history and the opportunity to sample Harrogate's sulphurous water.
TURKISH BATHS & HEALTH SPA - Parliament Street. Tel: 01423 556746. Go on, pamper yourself!
MERCER ART GALLERY - Swan Road. Tel: 01423 556188. Fine art collection plus travelling exhibitions.

Shopping
All the main shopping areas are within easy walking distance of the railway station, even if you're encumbered with packages on the way back. Affluent James Street has its apothesis in HOOPERS department store; on West Park OTTAWAY'S dispenses imaginative giftware which will go some way to diffusing awkward situations if you're late home. RICHARD AXE'S rare and out of print book shop can be found on Cheltenham Crescent; likewise BOOKS FOR ALL on Commercial Street which also hosts the aptly-named POMP & CIRCUMSTANCE classical CD shop and an excellent deli called THE CHEESEBOARD.

Connections
BUSES - useful links to towns no longer served by train such as Wetherby, Tadcaster, Ripon and Boroughbridge. The bus station conveniently adjoins the railway station Tel: 01423 566061 or 0870 608 2 608.
TAXIS - Blue Line. Tel: 01423 530830.

Hellifield *Map 5*

The village declined with its railway station, but new housing on the site of the L&Y yard may inject fresh impetus, especially if a proper service can be introduced over the line to Clitheroe, Blackburn and beyond. Quaint wooden fish & chip shop in village centre.

Walking

Follow the Ribble Way downstream to Clitheroe or upstream to Giggleswick (16 miles). Cross Otterburn Moor to Airton and continue up the Pennine Way to Malham (8 miles).

Horton-in-Ribblesdale *Map 9*

Base camp for the Three Peaks, and a stopping off point on the Pennine Way, and more recently devised, Ribble Way. So at most times of the year it hooches with folk in cagoules wilting under the weight of enormous haversacks. Yet, apart from the picturesque narrow bridges which span the Ribble and Brants Gill, and the ancient, largely Norman church of St Oswald's, the village itself is not that intrinsically attractive, a good proportion of the local economy being derived from quarrying and lorry driving.

Accommodation, Eating & Drinking

PEN-Y-GHENT CAFE - a mecca for walkers, cavers, cyclists and visitors who value the enthusiasm and local knowledge of the staff who know how to cater for hungry appetites born of the fells: tea comes, for instance, scalding hot in pint mugs! The cafe also stocks an excellent range of Dales literature and guides. Open daily - except for Tuesdays. Tel: 01729 860333.

CROWN HOTEL - 3 minutes walk from station. Tel: 01729 860209. Very comfortable country inn. Food and accommodation.

BLIND BECK TEA ROOMS - farmhouse tea rooms by railway bridge at north end of village.

Walking

Penyghent (2 miles) and Ingleborough (4 miles) can be comfortably reached from Horton station. The Ribble Way is also worth considering.

Keighley *Map 3*

An immediately likeable town with few airs and graces, Keighley's prosperity was built on textiles and engineering, activities which continue to play a role in the town's economy. Peter Black, suppliers of clothing and other goods to Marks & Spencer, have premises overlooking the railway. Stone predominates in the town centre and there are many dignified buildings in the main thoroughfares, like the handsome Edwardian public library in North Street.

Eating & Drinking

Keighley is the home of Timothy Taylor's prize-winning ales and many characterful pubs serve their output, as do the buffet cars on the KWVR. There also seem to be more fish & chip shops than you'd find in Morecambe or Bridlington.

Shopping

For a town of its size Keighley is a surprisingly good shopping centre, and Cavendish Street, the first street of shops you reach from the station, has an unusual canopy overhanging its pavement on one side. The Airedale Shopping Centre houses most of the better known retail chains, there's a market hall, and several factory shops such as Peter Black.

Things to Do

KEIGHLEY & WORTH VALLEY RAILWAY - Keighley station. One of the longest established, most successful and most charming of Britain's preserved steam railways, the KWVR extends for almost five miles up the narrow valley of the River Worth. Stations include: Ingrow, with its vintage carriage exhibition; Oakworth, star of the film *The Railway Children*; Haworth, centre of Bronteland and location of the line's locomotive depot; and Oxenhope, the delightful terminus in an edge of the moors location. Trains run at weekends throughout the year and daily in the summer. Tel: 01535 645214 or 647777.

Walking

Follow the Worth Way (5 miles linear or 11 miles circular) waymarked paths linking Keighley with Haworth and Oxenhope. Leaflets available from the Tourist Information Centre at Haworth - Tel: 01535 42329.

Kirkby Stephen *Map 13*

"A place for licking wounds and replenishing stores" wrote Wainwright in the guidebook to his own "Coast to Coast" walk. Settle & Carlisle travellers will tend to see it from a different point of view, and are likely to be put off by the thought of a long walk along a busy road without a pavement for part of the way. But the occasional bus meets the train and there are taxis to be hired and, in many respects, Kirkby Stephen is every bit as interesting to explore as Appleby. The town is blessed with a good proportion of handsome buildings in a wide variety of architectural styles and periods. Look out for the Temperance Hall with its slightly primitive figure of the Goddess of Temperance dressed in blue above the doorway, and the old butter market standing very fetchingly in front of the imposing parish church, known as 'the cathedral of the dale'. Many of the buildings are built from the local brockram stone, an unusual mixture of limestone and sandstone which takes on a rosy hue when the sun shines. Away from the bustle of main street there are quiet walks to be had beside the River Eden, which can be crossed by a quaint pack horse bridge.

Kirkby Stephen

Accommodation, Eating & Drinking

KINGS ARMS - Market Street. Meals and accommodation. Tel: 017683 71378.

PENNINE HOTEL - Market Street. Meals and accommodation. Tel: 017683 71382.

YOUTH HOSTEL - Market Street. Tel: 017683 71793.

OLD FORGE RESTAURANT - North Road. Open Tue-Sun evenings. Tel: 017683 71832.

COAST TO COAST - fish & chip shop named after Wainwright's walk. Eat in or take-away. Tel: 017683 71194. Parrots fly surrealy in and out of the roof of the house across the road! *Lots of tea-rooms too.*

Shopping

The town is the recognised shopping centre for a wide district. Monday has been market day since 1361, and the stalls stand in an attractive setting overlooked by St Stephens. There are several craft and antique shops, a gallery and a bookshop. Thursday is early closing and there are branches of Barclays and HSBC banks.

Things to Do

TOURIST INFORMATION - Market Square. Tel: 017683 71199. (Closed in winter). *www.visiteden.co.uk*

Walking

Get a copy of the "Stepping Over Stone" walk leaflet from the TIC and follow this 13 mile circular route via Crosby Garrett encountering both the Settle & Carlisle and old NER railways en route. Kirkby Stephen is often used as a starting point for guided walks.

Connections

BUSES - services to/from Brough, Sedburgh, Barnard Castle and Ravenstonedale. Tel: 0870 608 2 608. On Tuesdays in Summer Cumbria Classic Coaches operate a vintage bus service between Kirkby Stephen railway station, Hawes and Ribblehead. Tel: 015396 23254.

TAXIS - Tel: 017683 71741 or 71682.

Knaresborough *Map 19*

A 'story-book town' according to British Railways 1952 *Holiday Guide to Eastern England,* Knaresborough could easily be overawed by its proximity to Harrogate and York, but it has a trick up its sleeve in the form of the Nidd Gorge. It is twinned with Bebra, a German railway town. In summer you can row skiffs on the river under the ramparts of the ruined castle and pass beneath the viaduct - ikon of many an LNER poster - and marvel at Pevsner's untypically misguided appraisal. On winter lunchtimes, during school term, the market place fills with kilted schoolgirls, to the gratification of dull, middle-aged travel writers, deluded that they've fallen upon a remake

continued overleaf

Knaresborough

Karen Tanguy

continued from page 49
of *Brigadoon* and apt to break into spontaneous paeans of appreciation.

Accommodation
DOWER HOUSE HOTEL - Bond End. Tel: 01423 863302. Comfortable Best Western hotel with leisure club.

Eating & Drinking
OFF THE RAILS - bistro attractively incorporated into the fabric of the railway station. Tel: 01423 866587.
MARIOS - Waterside. Tel: 01423 863117. Award-winning Italian nestling picturesquely under the railway viaduct. Ice cream too!
DRAKES - Silver Street. Archetypal Yorkshire fish & chip restaurant and take-away. Tel: 01423 864864.
BLIND JACK'S - Market Place. Tel: 01423 869148. Lively CAMRA recommended pub featuring the output of many Yorkshire breweries.
FARM DAIRY - Market Place. Tel: 01423 865027. Deli & cheesemonger. Rolls made to measure & fresh salads.

Shopping
A market town since the 14th century, Knaresborough offers shopping in less frenetic circumstances than Harrogate or York. Good pies from ROBINSON'S on Kirkgate, a wide choice of bottled beer from BEER RITZ in the Market Place, Farrah's Original Harrogate Toffee from YE OLDEST CHEMIST SHOPPE.

Things to Do
TOURIST INFORMATION - Castle Courtyard. Tel: 01423 866886.
MOTHER SHIPTON'S CAVE - Tel: 01423 864600.Long-established visitor attraction commemorating the 16th century prophetess Mother Shipton. Also features a petrifying well. Audio tours, riverside walks, tea rooms and shop.
CASTLE & MUSEUM - Castle Yard. Tel: 01423 556188. Thomas Beckett's assasins fled here in 1170. The museum celebrates Knaresborough's associations with the Civil War.
BOAT HIRE - Marigolds. Tel: 01423 869773. Blenkhorns. Tel: 01423 862105/865654.

Connections
BUSES - Tel: 01423 566061. Useful links with Boroughbridge and Ripon.

Lancaster *Map 8*

Barely a brick in sight in compact, handsome, stone-built Lancaster. City status was only conferred as recently as 1937, but its pedigree goes back to the Norman Conquest; and in its heyday as a Georgian port, connected with the slave trade, has bequeathed a legacy of elegant architecture. Trade and commerce have ebbed away from Lancaster's waterfront, but from the banks of the Lune it still looks an imposing sort of place, crowned by a skyline of turrets, battlements, domes, spires, clocktowers and miscellaneous perpendicular landmarks, which provoke the urge to explore it to the full.

Accommodation
ROYAL KINGS ARMS HOTEL - Market Street. Three star hotel handy for station. Tel: 01524 32451.

Eating & Drinking
JOHN O' GAUNT - Market Street. Tel: 01524 65356. Busy, bawdy, brilliant - all a town pub should be. Jennings and guest beers plus bar lunches.
IL BISTRO MORINI - Sun Street (off Market Street). Tel: 01524 846252. Award-winning Italian open for lunch Thur-Sat and dinner daily ex Sun.
SIMPLY FRENCH - St George's Quay. Tel: 01524 843199. French cooking on the *rive gauche* of the Lune. Thur-Sat lunches, Tue-Sun dinners.
WATER WITCH - Aldcliffe Road. Imaginative canalside conversion from former boat horse stables. Local beers and excellent food. Tel: 01524 63828.

Shopping
A good, pedestrianised centre for shopping within just a few minutes reach of the railway station. Modern market hall open Monday - Saturday. Farmers Market on the 2nd Wednesday in the month. Many characterful individual shops - look out for Atkinson's tea and coffee emporium on, appropriately enough, China Street, which looks as though only the staff have changed since it was established in 1837.

Things to Do
TOURIST INFORMATION - Castle Hill. Tel: 01524 32878. Less than 5 minutes walk from the station and adjacent to the castle.
MARITIME MUSEUM - St George's Quay. An exhibition of the Port of Lancaster housed in an elegant 18th century Custom House. Open daily. Tel: 01524 64637.
WILLIAMSON PARK & ASHTON MEMORIAL - Lancaster's crowning glory is a folly built in 1909 in the grounds of a splendid Victorian park. The memorial and the grounds are open daily and attractions include a butterfly house and pavilion tea rooms. Entrance about 1 mile east of the station. Tel: 01524 33318.
Many of the city's most historic buildings: the castle, Catholic cathedral, old town hall, priory and judge's lodging, are open to the public. Full details from the TIC.

Walking
Try the fascinating "Maritime Trail". Descriptive booklets are available from various shops, museums and the TIC to this tour of Lancaster's days as an important port. The full walk will take two or three hours to complete.

Cycling
CYCLEPOINT - Platform 3, railway station. Tel: 01524 389410. Splendid budget bike-hire initiative to encourage cycling in an area blessed with traffic-free paths, notably the former railway lines to Morecambe, Glasson Dock and Caton and the Lancaster Canal towpath to Carnforth. Arrive by train and have a great day out!

Connections
BUSES - Tel: 0870 608 2 608.
TAXIS - Tel: 01524 848 848.

Langwathby *Map 15*

A stone's throw from the station, 17th century houses built from dark red local sandstone overlook the medieval village green. Children still dance round the maypole on the third Saturday in May. The bridge carrying the Alston-Penrith road across the River Eden was swept away by floods in 1968 and its temporary replacement is still there. The local farming economy is boosted by an animal feeds mill.

Eating, Drinking & Accommodation
BRIEF ENCOUNTER - charming cafe housed in former booking hall on the station. Tel: 01768 881902.
SHEPHERD'S INN - village centre. Nice village pub offering food and accommodation. Tel: 01768 881335.

Things to Do
EDEN OSTRICH WORLD - village centre. Tel: 01768 881771. Fun for all the family, open all year round.
ACORN BANK - 5 miles south-east of Langwathby. Open daily April to October. National Trust gardens. Tel: 017683 61893.

HAZEL DENE - Culgaith. Nursery and tea rooms; the latter adjacent to level crossing and decorated with railwayana. Tel: 01768 88252.
LITTLE SALKELD WATERMILL - a mile north-east of Langwathby. Delightful working watermill. Tours Mon, Tues & Thurs March to October. Mill shop open Mon-Fri all year round. Tel: 01768 881523.

Walking

Leaflets describing walks in the Langwathby area available from the village stores or Appleby TIC.

Connections

BUSES - links to/from Penrith and Alston in the summer months. Tel: 0870 608 2 608.

Lazonby *Map 16*

Famous for its Autumn sheep sales, Lazonby is an otherwise peaceful village situated beside the River Eden. It has close connections with Kirkoswald to which it is linked by a fine 18th century river bridge. Lazonby's most significant building is the Victorian church, which stands on a mound overlooking the station, but the circular cattle mart is also well worth going to see, especially if it's Wednesday and there happens to be a sale on. Facilities include a couple of pubs, a Co-op and a post office. Accommodation available from the CROWN INN at Kirkoswald on the opposite side of the Eden - Tel: 01768 898435.

Leeds *Map 1*

A unexpectedly fascinating city, buoyed up in recent years by its success as a centre of commerce and finance: though we must credit the Victorians for the greater part of the city's fabric; masterpieces like the Town Hall and the Corn Exchange - both the work of local architect, Cuthbert Broderick - and the Parish Church would grace any city. Likewise Kirkgate Market and the arcades off Briggate. But it's perhaps along the banks of the Aire that the greatest revelation is exposed to visitors. No longer working for a living in a barge-busy, cargo-carrying sense, the river nevertheless retains a commercial dignity in which its handsome warehouses, converted now into restaurants, hotels, offices and residential properties, reflect their former grandeur with their integrity intact.

Accommodation

THE QUEENS - City Square (adjoing railway station). Tel: 0113 243 1323. Majestic former railway hotel dating from 1937 when it was opened with a flourish by the LMS Railway , a huge Art Deco building of Portland stone, demonstrating pre-war confidence in rail travel - it was apparently Britain's first air-conditioned hotel!

Leeds

Eating & Drinking

LA COMIDA - Mill Hill (2 minutes walk from station - bear right at foot of station steps) Tel: 0113 244 0500. Lively Spanish/Italian restaurant run by a football-mad exile from Barcelona.
DIMITRI'S - Dock Street (approx 8 minutes walk from station to south of Leeds Bridge) Tel: 0113 246 0339. Stylish Greek taverna and tapas bar - offshoot of a similarly successful operation in Manchester.
POOL COURT AT 42. - The Calls. Michelin-starred restaurant offering aperitifs on a balcony over the Aire, an interior decor not unlike a classic ocean liner and cooking to match. Tel: 0113-244-4242.
WHITELOCKS - Turk's Head Yard, Briggate. Classic, unspoilt Victorian city pub. Tel: 0113 245 3950.

Things to Do

TOURIST INFORMATION - City Station. Tel: 0113 242 5242. Well-appointed information centre ideally placed for rail visitors to the city.
ROYAL ARMOURIES - Tel: 08700 344 344. Prestigious visitor centre devoted to the history of arms and warfare, about quarter of an hour's walk from the station.
CITY ART GALLERY - The Headrow. Tel: 0113-247-8248.
Out of town attractions, a short bus or taxi ride from the station, include: KIRKSTALL ABBEY & ABBEY HOUSE MUSEUM (Tel: 0113 230 5492); ARMLEY MILLS (Tel: 0113 263 7861) and THWAITE MILLS (Tel: 0113 249 6453) industrial museums; THACKRAY MUSEUM (Tel: 0113 244 4343); MIDDLETON RAILWAY (Tel: 0113 271 0320) and many others: further details of all these from the Tourist Information Centre.

Shopping

Shop 'til you drop' is Leeds' subliminal message, but then after all this is the place where Michael Marks set up his Penny Bazaar in 1884, so we should have known it would come to this. GRANARY WHARF is located in the 'Dark Arches' beneath the railway station, though redevelopment and (one suspects) an commensurate increase in rent, has rid it of the 'New Age' atmosphere which formerly prevailed so successfully. Elsewhere, mainstream Leeds shops with brio in the VICTORIA QUARTER, the ARCADES off Briggate and amidst the oval splendours of the CORN EXCHANGE. KIRKGATE MARKET dates from 1863, a huge indoor market hall of considerable atmosphere.

Walking

The WATERFRONT HERITAGE TRAIL stretches for 8 miles along the Aire from Rodley to Thwaite Mills, and it's disappointing that neither extremity is close to a handily placed railway station, but naturally there are bus links (see below) and the trail itself can be thoroughly recommended, whether you walk it in one fell swoop, or in more leisurely stages. A fine guidebook to the trail is available from the Tourist Information Centre. Of equal interest - but a less daunting 3 miles in length - is the HISTORIC PLAQUES TRAIL which introduces you to some of Leeds' most interesting buildings, events and personalities: again call in at the TIC for a map and leaflet.

Connections

Local bus/rail travel details on 0113 245 7676.

Long Preston *Map 5*

They still dance annually around the maypole in Long Preston, though the days of calico making and cattle trading are long gone. The permanently busy A65 tends to detract from what would otherwise be a picturesque village with its fair share of fine buildings, notably the almshouses overlooking the railway.

Accommodation, Eating & Drinking

MAYPOLE INN - village green. Muzak-free country pub offering good food and a thoughtful choice of beers, including the redoubtable Timothy Taylors and Moorhouses of Burnley. Accommodation as well - Tel: 01729 840219.

Morecambe *Map 8*

Once variously celebrated as the 'Sunset Coast' and 'Naples of the North', Morecambe has latterly come down to earth with a bump, perhaps being more accurately described as a *nipple* of the north now. Yet Morecambe's manfully trying to drag its arthritic limbs into a new millennium, and the Urban Splash plans for the Midland Hotel could well result in a dramatic transformation.
THE STATION - Ansells Big Steak & Wacky Warehouse pub housed in one wing of the Midland Railway's former 'Promenade' station.
BRUCCIANI'S - Marine Road. Italian ice cream cafe.
continued overleaf

G A Z E T T E E R

continued from page 51
ATKINSONS - Albert Road. Classic seaside fish & chips.
TOURIST INFORMATION - Promenade 'station'. Tel: 01524 582808.
FESTIVAL MARKET - traditional market relocated on the site of Promenade station's once imposing platforms, much to the chagrin of true railway lovers. Open Tues, Thur, Sat & Sun.

Poppleton *Map 20*

Old maps show two distinctive communities: Nether Poppleton, where a ferry operated across the Ouse; and Upper Poppleton grouped about a green close to the railway. But explosions of housing from the 1960s onwards have somewhat diluted the picturesque appeal, despite the survival of a maypole.

Accommodation, Eating & Drinking

THE RED LION - Boroughbridge Road, Upper Poppleton. Tel: 01904 781141. Motel-style pub with en suite rooms.
WETHERBY WHALER - Ings Lane, Nether Poppleton. Tel:01904 784500. Modern fish & chip restaurant/take-away in the Harry Ramsden mould located on the A1237 between the Harrogate railway and the East Coast Main Line.

Ribblehead *Map 10*

Not so much a settlement, more the source of its eponymous river in a wild, moorland setting overlooked by Whernside and Ingleborough. Informal camping and parking is available beside the B6255 and this activity tends to intrude on the sense of wilderness at the height of the season. But caves and limestone pavements lie within easy reach of the station and you can soon escape from the hot-dog stands and unambitious crowds.

Eating & Drinking

The STATION INN is a homely little pub offering food and accommodation either on bed & breakfast terms or in their adjoining bunkhouse. Tel: 01542 41274.

Walking

The classic 'must do' walk for anyone remotely interested in the Settle & Carlisle and its landscapes starts at Ribblehead and finishes at Dent. Though not waymarked (it wouldn't be because we 'invented' it!) it's easy to follow and marked on Maps 10 & 11. Walk down the station drive and take the track across Batty Moss running parallel to the viaduct. Continue past Blea Moor signal box, crossing the line by way of Force Gill aqueduct. Where the Dales Way bears left over the flank of Whernside, bear right and keep to the track which runs between the spoil heaps and past the air shafts over the tunnel top. Keep to the path as it descends through conifer plantations to join the road by Dent Head Viaduct. Continue to Cowgill and Dent station. Distance 7 miles; allow 3-4 hours.

Connections

BUSES - on summer Tuesdays Cumbria Classic Coaches operate one of their charming vintage vehicles on an afternoon link with Hawes and Kirkby Stephen which would make an entertaining round trip returning by rail from KS - Tel: 015396 23254. On summer Sundays you can travel on a Keighley & Distric bus sponsored by North Yorkshire County Council to Hawes, Wensleydale and Richmond - Tel: 0870 608 2 608.

Saltaire *Map 2*

Second stop out from Leeds and already there's every temptation to go no further. Barges laden with Alpaca wool once plied between Liverpool docks and Sir Titus Salt's somewhat immodestly named mill village of Saltaire. Now, inevitably, the emphasis is on tourism, but in an uncanny way, the model community - a sort of Yorkshire Bournville or Port Sunlight - erected by the philanthropic Mr Salt for his workforce, absorbs the usual excesses and compromises of the tourist culture, successfully maintaining its veracity. Salt's gargantuan five storey mill, strategically located between the already well established canal and the new railway, was post-industrially resurrected by Jonathan Silver before his untimely death, and is now a flourishing cornucopia of style and enterprise, featuring permanent exhibitions of local boy made good, David Hockney. Everything is done in the best possible taste, with flair and imagination, and Saltaire cannot be recommended too highly for a day out or, indeed, a lengthier stay.

Accommodation

BEETIES - Victoria Road. Tel: 01274 595988. Award-winning accommodation and stylish restaurant.

Eating & Drinking

SALT'S DINER - Salt's Mill. Tel: 01274 530533. Open daily 10am-6pm (last food orders 4.30pm). Atmospheric cafe/restaurant serving inexpensive quality food. True to the Hockney theme, even the paper napkins and crockery feature his famous Dachshund doodle.

Saltaire

CAFE IN TO THE OPERA - Salts Mill. Tel: 01274 531163. Open Weds-Suns. Splendid new third floor eating area in an operatic setting. Rigoletto with your ravioli!
VILLAGE BAKERY & CAFE - Victoria Road. Tel: 01274 533505. Basement cafe offering delicious, made on the premises, food.
VICTORIA FISHERIES - adjacent station. Tel: 01274 585000. Fish & chips as only Yorkshire knows how.

Things to Do

ORGAN & HARMONIUM MUSEUM - Victoria Road. Open daily ex Fri & Sat. 11am-4pm.
SHIPLEY GLEN TRAMWAY - 5 minutes walk from the station. Usually operating on weekends and bank holidays throughout the year. Tel: 01274 589010.
TOURIST INFORMATION - Victoria Street (adjacent to station). Tel: 01274 774993. Local information housed in gift shop.

Shopping

SALTS MILL overflows with stylish outlets including a gallery where you can buy prints, postcards and art books, a bookshop where titles are wonderfully displayed face up on tables and not shyly on shelves, a home-furnishing shop of considerable appeal; clothes, ceramics, carpets, a photographic gallery, a florists etc, etc; all done with the most amazing brio and elan. Across the railway there are antique shops and art galleries.

Walking

Towpath walks along the Leeds & Liverpool Canal. Turn to *Pearson's Canal Companion: Pennine Waters* for inspiration! Tel: 01788 546692.

Settle *Map 9*

People tend to use Settle as a launch pad for the railway and so miss much of its intrinsic charm. In fact there are few Yorkshire market towns more captivating than this, and it would be a great pity for you to see no more of it than the view from the carriage window. Settle's compact streets are squeezed between the east bank of the Ribble and a huge limestone outcrop known as the Castleberg. A steep path zig-zags to the top from which you can see the little town spread out like something on a model railway. From the market square, where Pennine Motor Services buses stop to pick up and set down, and the mountain bikes lie stacked, Oxbridge fashion, outside Ye Olde Naked Man Cafe, you can trace the tight-knit streets and alleys, charting their seemingly haphazard course about the purlieus of the town. Elgar was a regular visitor to Settle on account of his friendship with a local doctor, so perhaps the Yorkshire landscape, as well as Worcestershire and Herefordshire, inspired his muse.

Accommodation, Eating & Drinking

YE OLDE NAKED MAN - Market Place. Formerly an inn dating back to 1663. Now a pleasant cafe with an adjoining baker's shop - good for making up picnics. Tel: 01729 823230..
THE GOLDEN LION HOTEL - Duke Street. Tel: 01729 822203. Town centre 17th century coaching inn with en suite accommodation. Thwaites ales and bar meals.
ROYAL OAK - Market Place. Another town centre pub offering meals and accommodation. Tel: 01729 822561.
FALCON MANOR HOTEL - Skipton Road (about 8 minutes walk from the station on the southern edge of the town). Tel: 01729 823814. Imposing Victorian hotel in its own grounds.

LITTLE HOUSE RESTAURANT - Duke Street. Tel: 01729 823963.
SHAMBLES FISH BAR - Market Place. Tel: 01729 822652. Excellent eat in/take-away fish & chips.

Things to Do

TOURIST INFORMATION - Town Hall. Tel: 01729 825192. *www.yorkshiredales.org*

Shopping

They've been holding a market here on Tuesdays since 1249. The stalls gather around the old 'shambles', an intriguing split-level building with cottages on the top storey and shops on two levels below. By and large, Settle's shops are run on the old-fashioned philosophy of courtesy and personal service. There are some truly excellent bakers and grocers, notably GLYNNS 'gold medal' bakery on Church Street, a stopping off point for many West Riding folk on their way to and from The Dales and The Lakes. As befits a town on the doorstep of The Dales there are several country pursuits shops, at least two of which specialise in climbing and caving equipment. Wednesday is early closing and there are branches of NatWest, Lloyds TSB and HSBC banks. On the northern outskirts of town, WATERSHED MILL has been renovated to house a variety of speciality outlets including clothes, crafts, golf equipment, Yorkshire beers, a coffee shop and (or so we were promised as we went to press) a working scale model of Settle station - Tel: 01729 825539. BOOTH'S supermarket, which lies on the Giggleswick side of the railway, comes as a refreshing change to the big supermarket chains and offers, amongst many other delights, a comprehensive range of bottled beer.

Walking

Numerous possibilities suggest themselves for walks based on Settle: the Ribble Valley, Stainforth Scar, Malham etc. Try the TIC for local walks leaflets or join one of the guided walks from the train.

Connections

The distinctive orange and black Leyland Nationals of PENNINE MOTOR SERVICES link Settle with various other towns and villages not connected to the railway. Tel: 01756 795515.
SETTLE TAXIS - Tel: 01729 824824.

Skipton

Karen Tanguy

Skipton *Map 4*

You can easily run out of superlatives with old 'Sheep Town'. It's straddled the Aire Gap since the 7th century, and if our needs differ somewhat from the days of the packhorse, Skipton still has the knack of seeing to them in a spirited manner. The well-appointed station sets the tone, and the best approach to town is by way of the well-surfaced Leeds & Liverpool towpath (go straight over the road from the station forecourt up to the swing-bridge and turn right), a traffic-free entry into Skipton past the sort of mills upon which its industrial economy was founded. The largest of them now produces greetings cards, but was once renowned as the home of 'Sylko' sewing thread. A branch of the canal pokes its liquid finger up to the bosky castle ramparts, and having reached Mill Bridge, you can make a grand entry into the town at the top of its broad, market stall-filled High Street.

Accommodation

BLACK HORSE HOTEL - High Street. Something of a Skipton instituition, this former coaching inn offers accommodation and a wide range of meals, including breakfasts for non-residents. Tel: 01756 792145.
HANOVER INTERNATIONAL HOTEL - Keighley Road. Comfortable, modern canalside hotel with fitness club and brasserie restaurant. Tel: 01756 700100.

Eating & Drinking

EASTWOODS - Keighley Road. Tel: 01756 795458. Canalside fish & chip shop and restaurant.
BIZZIE LIZZIES - Belmont Bridge. Ditto above. Tel: 01756 701131.
THE NARROW BOAT - Victoria Street (off Coach Street). Tel: 01756 797922. CAMRA recommended pub offering lunchtime food and an interesting variety of beers including many Yorkshire-brewed ales.
WOOLLY SHEEP INN - Sheep Street. Tel: 01756 700966. Lively town centre pub offering a wide range of bar food and Timothy Taylor beers. En suite accommodation as well.

Things to Do

TOURIST INFORMATION - Coach Street. Tel: 01756 792809.
SKIPTON CASTLE - superb 11th century fortification, though much domesticised down the years. Open daily from 10am (2pm on Sundays). Tel: 01756 792442.
EMBSAY & BOLTON ABBEY RAILWAY - located at Embsay, 2 miles east of Skipton, bus connections. Delightful steam railway originally part of the Midland Railway's Skipton-Ilkley line. Now extends for three and a half miles between Embsay and Bolton Abbey, just over a mile from the famous abbey ruins. Operates weekends throughout the year together with selected weekdays in summer. Talking timetable on 01756 795189; other information on 01756 710614. Well-stocked railway bookshop on Embsay station. Bus links from Skipton (see below).
PENNINE CRUISERS - Coach Street. Tel: 01756 795478. Day boats for hire along a 17 mile lock-free stretch of the Leeds & Liverpool Canal.
PENNINE BOAT TRIPS - Coach Street. Tel: 01756 790829. Public trips along the canal, usually daily in summer.

Shopping

Skipton is an excellent shopping centre and its popularity has attracted big names like Rackhams, Laura Ashley and Edinburgh Woollen Mill to open branches here. Market stalls line the High Street on Mondays, Wednesdays, Fridays and Saturdays. Many alleyways issue from the High Street, leading to interesting courtyards, most notably CRAVEN COURT, an alley opening out into an airy rectangle covered by a graceful canopy of cast iron and glass. As well as the chain stores there are lots of individual shops of character, none more so than STANFORTH'S 'celebrated pork pie establishment' (on Mill Bridge - Tel: 01756 793477) where the pies come warm and the jelly explodes in your mouth (and all over your clothes if you're not careful!).

Connections

PENNINE MOTORS serve Malham (for The Cove, Tarn & Gordale Scar) and Embsay (for the steam railway). Timings on 01756 795515.
TAXIS - Station Taxis, Tel: 01756 796666.
BICYCLE HIRE - The Bicycle Shop, Water Street. Tel: 01756 794386.

GAZETTEER

York *Map 20*

Chocolates, history and railways are the gifts that York brings to the party; more particularly the venerated brand names of Rowntrees and Terrys, the Vikings and the Romans, and the murky financial speculations of a draper called Hudson who infamously desired to 'mak all t' railways cum to York'. Only Bath and Stratford-on-Avon can seriously hold a candle to it in terms of tourism outside the capital, and so it pays to see York in its quieter moments: an early morning circumnavigation of the walls, perhaps; an out of season jolly on the Ouse; or, best of all, the ascent to the top of the Minster tower.

Accommodation

LE MERIDIEN - Station Road (direct access from station platform). Tel: 01904 653681. One of the great 'railway hotels', built in1878 using Scarborough brick and Tadcaster limestone in deference to its location beside the city's medieval wall. Well worth patronising - even if the room rate is more than you're used to - for its ambience of burnished pomp. At the least treat yourself to morning coffee, an open sandwich, or afternoon tea in the lounge; whilst a more formal luncheon or dinner in the Rose Room Restaurant - once featured in LNER poster campaigns - will leave a lasting memory.

DEAN COURT HOTEL - Duncombe Place. Tel: 01904 625082. Best Western hotel in the shadow of the Minster.

YORK BACKPACKERS - Micklegate (5 minutes walk from the station). Tel: 01904 627720. Budget accommodation for all ages on one of York's most handsome thoroughfares.

HOTEL RESERVATIONS - useful kiosk facility on Platform 5 for instant accommodation bookings to suit all budgets. Tel: 0800 371321.

Eating & Drinking

BLAKE HEAD CAFE - Micklegate. Tel: 01904 623767. Admirable vegetarian cafe to rear of discount bookshop, 5 minutes walk from the station. Friendly staff, a haven of calm, and nourishing food served in stylish surrounds.

THE BLUE BICYCLE - Fossgate. Tel: 01904 673990. Highly regarded restaurant located in former house of ill repute overlooking the River Foss.

CAFE CONCERTO - High Petergate. Tel: 01904 610478. Bohemian bistro with music theme adjacent to the Minster.

BETTYS - St Helen's Square. Tel: 01904 659142. A Yorkshire institution, one of just five branches of the celebrated tea room chain. This branch features interior designs inspired by the SS *Queen Mary* in 1936. Open from 9am-pm daily. Regular pianist accompaniment to aid the digestive juices. Much competition for tables at busy times; Little Bettys in nearby Stonegate providing a source of relief.

THREE LEGGED MARE - High Petergate. Tel: 01904 638246. York Brewery outlet blissfully free from electronic impedimenta and offering an enjoyable, if limited, choice of bar lunches along with its lovely beers.

PUCCINO'S - Railway Station. An impish sense of fun pervades Puccino's cafes, from the paper napkins through the crockery to the bottled water: 'flat' or 'bumpy'! This one, furthermore, gives a grandstand view of the main through platforms, for it is housed in former signal box accessed from the station's main footbridge. Tel: 01904 625556. Take-away orders on 01904 628811.

Shopping

An infinity of shops to keep the womenfolk content while you wander round the NRM. You might also like to know that the YORK ANTIQUE CENTRE (Tel: 01904 641445) on Lendal (1st right over Lendal Bridge) features one or two dealers in railway memorabilia, though this in no way makes up for the sad demise of British Rail's 'Collector's Corner'.

Things to Do

TOURIST INFORMATION - Railway Station/De Grey Rooms. Tel: 01904 621756.

NATIONAL RAILWAY MUSEUM - Leeman Road. Tel: 01904 621621. Where more appropriate to house the national collection of railway locomotives, rolling stock, artefacts and memorabilia than a former goods shed and motive power depot? 50A to aficionados of the old school! Former habitues may miss the soot and smoke, but this is definitely a museum with something for everyone. Open daily, admission free, just 5 minutes walk from the station or catch the regular Road Train link.

YORK MODEL RAILWAY - Railway Station. Tel: 01904 630169. Large and colourful model railway layout housed in former station tearoom, well worth visiting between real trains. Open daily, small admission charge.

JORVIK - Coppergate. Tel: 01904 543403. Popular, ground-breaking reconstruction of Viking York. Open daily.

YORKBOAT - Lendal Bridge. Tel: 01904 628324. River trips on the Ouse from February through to November.

OPEN TOP BUSES - frequent departures daily from the railway station. An easy and enjoyable introduction to the city. Tel: 01904 655585.

YORK MINSTER - Deangate. Tel: 01904 557216. Simply awe-inspiring, one of Christendom's great churches. Audio and guided tours, donations sought.

BREWERY TOUR - Toft Green (off Micklegate within 5 minutes walk of the station). As an enthusiasm for beer often runs concurrently with a love of railways, we thought you might enjoy a visit to the York Brewery Company's premises which offers guided tours Mon-Sat for a small admission charge, largely offset by the lure of a free pint's sample. Tel: 01904 621162. A small shop offers an appealing range of merchandise.

Connections

BUSES - Tel: 01904 551400.

TAXIS - Streamline. Tel: 01904 638833.

BIKE HIRE - Europcar, Platform 1, Railway Station. Tel: 01904 656161. Ideal point of departure for exploring 'Britain's Best Cycling City' by bicycle.

York

Information

Using This Guide

Twenty 'one inch to one mile' maps portray the route of the Leeds-Morecambe (1-8), Settle & Carlisle (9-17) and Leeds-Harrogate-York (18-20) railways. Each map is accompanied by a running commentary on matters historical, topographical and related to railway operation. Emphasis is given to the northward journey in each case, but the details are equally relevant for travel in the opposite direction.

Towards the rear of the guide a Gazetteer gives details of most of the places served by trains on these lines. Stations serving places without an entry in the Gazetteer are deemed to lack any significant facilities for rail travellers. The Gazetteer gives a brief 'pen portrait' of each place together with itemised information on places to eat and find accommodation, visitor centres, shopping, walking and bus connections. Where accuracy is essential to the planning of an itinerary you are urged to contact the telephone number quoted or the local Tourist Information Centre for up to date details.

Scheduled Services

Day to day services on the lines covered by this guide are part of the Regional Railways North East franchise, operated by Arriva Trains Northern as we went to press, but due to be combined into a new 'Northern' franchise in September 2004. Current service levels on the Leeds to Morecambe line consist of five return trips Monday-Saturday and a reduced Sunday timetable. On the Leeds-Settle-Carlisle line there are eight or nine weekday return trips depending on the time of year as well as Sunday services as well. On summer Sundays two additional services work on to the Settle & Carlisle line from Lancashire over the Ribble Valley Line via Hellifield. Between Leeds/Bradford and Skipton there is an intensive electric suburban service. Between Leeds and York via Knaresborough the weekday service operates half-hourly, and hourly on to York; on Sundays the service is hourly throughout.

The average journey time between Leeds and Morecambe is two hours, between Settle and Carlisle it is around an hour and a half. Leeds to York via Harrogate takes an hour and ten minutes minutes. Pocket timetables covering all these services are available widely or telephone National Rail Enquiries on 08457 484950 or *www.nationalrail.co.uk*

Charter Trains

Several operators run charter trains regularly over the Settle & Carlisle with either steam (S) or diesel (D) locomotives. The following list is not exhaustive but it represents the companies whose trains are most often to be seen on the line. In most cases their trains run from centres far removed from the line: viz London & the Home Counties, The West Country, West Midlands etc. Look out for their advertisements in the National Press and railway interest magazines, or contact them direct for advance details of their forthcoming trips.

GARSDALE RAIL TOURS (D) - 01539 620586

GREEN EXPRESS (D) - 01484 422920 *www.greenexpressrailtours.me.uk*

HERTFORDSHIRE RAILTOURS (D) - 01438 812125 *www.traintrips.co.uk*

PATHFINDER TOURS (S/D) - 01453 835414 *www.toursatpathfinder.freeserve.co.uk*

PAST TIME RAIL (S/D) - 01543 411971 *www.past-time.co.uk*

STEAMY AFFAIRS (S) - 01553 828107 *www.steamyaffairs.net*

VSOE NORTHERN - Tel: 0161 831 7900 *www.orient-express.com*

Walking

A programme of guided walks by local experts operates from stations on the Leeds-Carlisle and Leeds-Morecambe lines throughout the year, mostly at weekends and also on some Wednesdays as well. Leaflets listing the programme of walks are widely distributed throughout the region. The walks vary from 12-18 miles in length, and some are tougher than others depending on the local terrain.

Bicycles

Space for bicycles is limited on the diesel units which provide most of the services, only an average of two spaces being available on a 'first-come, first-served' basis. On the Settle & Carlisle line Arriva Trains Northern currently ask that space is reserved in advance, either at a staffed station or via their telephone helpline on 0870 602 3322.

Tickets & Travelpasses

The following stations covered in this guide are staffed: Appleby, Bingley, Carlisle, Carnforth, Harrogate, Horsforth, Keighley, Lancaster, Leeds, Morecambe, Settle, Shipley, Skipton and York Elsewhere tickets must be purchased from the conductor on the train. All day to day services on the lines covered are standard class only. Groups of ten or more travelling together can discuss discounts with Arriva Trains Northern who also operate a helpline for disabled travellers on 08456 008 008.

Useful Contacts

SETTLE-CARLISLE PARTNERSHIP *www.settle-carlisle.co.uk* An excellent and topical website devoted to all aspects of the Settle & Carlisle providing up to date information and many useful links, including the Friends of the Settle-Carlisle Line.

ARRIVA TRAINS NORTHERN *www.arrivatrainsnorthern.co.uk* Current (and much respected) holders of the operating franchise but due for change in September 2004.

BRITRAIL - rail travel for overseas visitors. Visit *www.BritRail.net*

ACORP - Association of Community-Rail Partnerships. Tel: 01484 549737. *www.acorp.uk.com* Promotional group for rural railways supported by the Countryside Agency, SRA and ATOC.

WENSLEYDALE RAILWAY - now operating between Leyburn and Leeming Bar but with ambitions to re-open the full route between Garsdale (where it will connect with the Settle & Carlisle) and Northallerton. Tel: 08454 505474 *www.wensleydalerailway.com*

EDEN VALLEY RAILWAY - restoration of the former North Eastern Railway route between Appleby and Kirkby Stephen. Tel: 01228 512204 *www.evr.org.uk*

Themed, guided, inclusive holiday tours of the Settle & Carlisle are operated by:

TRACKS NORTH - 01539 824666.

INSIDE TRACK - 01442 872995.

Further Reading

The Story of the Settle-Carlisle Line by Houghton & Foster pub 1948 o/p

North of Leeds by P.E. Baughan pub 1966 o/p

The Little North Western Railway by Martin Bairstow ISBN 1 871944 21 X

Railways Around Harrogate (Vol 3) by Martin Bairstow ISBN 1 871944 18 X

Also by Michael Pearson

Iron Road to the Isles
ISBN 0 907864 87 2
Iron Road to the Highlands
ISBN 0 907864 93 7
Iron Road to Whisky Country
ISBN 0 907864 94 5
Iron Roads to the Far North & Kyle
ISBN 0907864 98 8
Railway Holiday in Scotland
ISBN 0 907864 90 2
Coming Up With the Goods
ISBN 0 907864 81 3
Me, My Morgan & The Midlands
ISBN 0 907864 95 3
Pearson's Canal Companions (9 vols)*
*Tel: 01788 546692 for details**

Acknowledgements

Grateful thanks to Arriva Trains Northern for their support in the preparation of this book, especially Tony Hargrave and Drew Haley. Special thanks also to guest photographers David Alison, Robert Armitstead, Bob Green and Peter J. Robinson whose work illuminates this volume. Thank you to Claire Lloyd-Raine for authorising an interior view of the Brief Encounter Buffet Room at Carnforth and to Will Hamer and his family of Cumbria Classic Coaches for making one of their charming vintage buses available for photography. Thanks to Frank Roach of the Highland Rail Partnership and John Yellowlees of ScotRail for their continued enthusiasm and belief and for allowing the *Iron Roads* brand to be exported to England. Thanks to Paul Salveson of ACORP for his support and networking. Multo grazie a Giampiero Logiudice e tutto nostro amicos a STIGE per loro totto bene lavoro. Thanks to Karen Tanguy and her increasing collection of millinery; to Eden for carrying the tripod and to Jackie and Tamar for home and hearth.